GOTCHA!

The Art of the Billboard

Edited by Wei Yew

© 1990

Published by Quon Editions © 1990
in association with Page One – The
Bookshop Pte. Ltd., Singapore.

Printed in Singapore by Tien Wah Press

First Edition 1990

Quon Editions
#203, 10107 – 115 Street
Edmonton, Alberta.
T5K 1T3 Canada.

Page One – The Bookshop Pte. Ltd.
6 Raffles Boulevard
#03–128 Marina Square
Singapore 0103

ISBN 0-9694432-1-8

GOTCHA!

The Art of the Billboard

Edited by Wei Yew

Quon Editions

Art Director
Wei Yew
Design & Production
Studio 3 Graphics
Cover Photography
Dwayne Brown
Billboard Photography
James Sew
Typographer
Contemporary Type
Printer
Tien Wah Press, Singapore

Contents

Since some of the billboards are quite specific in nature, the selected works are only roughly categorized in this contents page to facilitate quick reference and not intended as a definitive classification of billboards.

Preface

Billboards are very much a part of our lives. Unless one has lost the use of one's sight, it is impossible to avoid encountering a billboard or a transit ad-panel. We are confronted by these environmental 'scenics' on our way to and from work everyday.

While some people are opposed to the visual pollution of the environment caused by these monstrous hoardings, others seem to enjoy them as pieces of art that entertain during an otherwise boring freeway journey. There is a definite art to transforming a message onto a billboard that will instantly capture the attention of a driver travelling at 60 mph or more. I have found that the most effective billboards come from the controlled use of words and creative handling of graphics.

Transit shelter billboards and other panels that are found in public transit vehicles have a somewhat easier task of capturing the attention of commuters. Here, messages and graphics are assimilated at a more leisurely pace by a captive audience. Even so, many of the panels found in this publication are fine examples of simple and effective advertisement.

One person seems to have dominated the billboard scene here by his excellent works. Bob Kwait of Phillips-Ramsey Advertising and Public Relations, San Diego submitted, amongst other works, his well-known San Diego Zoo series (from page 136).

In light of the many bad billboards to be found, I can share the sentiments of those opposed to the proliferation of signs in our environment. However, I am also most impressed with the many creative billboards that we received. Such works should be permanently installed on a 100 mile highway dedicated to great billboards. Perhaps, one day such an open museum may be available for the preservation of effective billboard designs.

A word of thanks to the following people for their assistance:

All the designers who took time to send in their works;

Bob Kwait, San Diego for writing the introduction;

John Bilney of Mediacom, Toronto;

Pendar Zamani of Patrick Media Group, Los Angeles;

Vance & Greg Macdonald and Carey Twa of Hook Outdoor Advertising;

Bryon Peddie of Gallop + Gallop Advertising Inc.; and

Mary Yeow for organizing submission entries and tracking down the various resources.

Wei Yew

Bob Kwait

Bob Kwait is executive vice president/creative director at Phillips-Ramsey Advertising and Public Relations. He supervises and reviews all work conducted by the agency's creative department, and sits on the Phillips-Ramsey Board of Directors, Executive Committee, Operating Management Group, and Plans Board. Kwait joined the agency on March 1, 1978.

Prior to arriving at Phillips-Ramsey, Kwait was vice president/creative director at Wyse Advertising of Cleveland and senior vice president/ executive art director at Griswold-Eshleman, also of Cleveland. He graduated from Cooper School of Art in Cleveland and took classes in advanced design from the Cleveland Institute of Art.

Throughout his career, Kwait has executed outstanding advertising for a variety of challenging clients: the WD-40 Company, the San Diego Wild Animal park, the Del Mar Thoroughbred Club, Lynx Golf Incorporated, AirCal, B.F. Goodrich, Hoover Vacuum Cleaners, Vicorp Restaurants, Super Glue, Las Vegas Hilton, Diawa Fishing Tackle, and Stouffer Restaurants and Hotels.

Perhaps Kwait is best-known for his work for the San Diego Zoo. A three-part billboard series featuring "the snake that ate the cake" will be long-remembered by San Diego commuters, as will the open-mouthed alligator snapping "See You Later". His peers have honoured Kwait again and again for the billboard, television, and print he has created for what has become one of Phillips-Ramsey's showcase accounts.

In fact, to characterize Kwait as the "award-winningest" creative personality in San Diego risks no dissension from the city's artistic community. His office and home are lined with plaques, certificates, and statuettes from the One Show, New York Art Directors Show, the Beldings, ANDYS, ADDYS, OBIES, Homburgs, SanDis, London International Advertising Awards, and CLIOS. Kwait has been recognized among "America's 100 Outstanding Creative People" in a nation-wide poll of creative professionals conducted by AdDay/USA.

Introduction

In my opinion, outdoor advertising is the most difficult medium to do well. The person you're trying to reach is flying by your message at 60 mph. He's not going to stop his car and pull over to the side of the road to read your billboard. You've got about 4 seconds to get your point across.

To be intelligible under these conditions, you've got to have a simple visual and a short headline. The idea should be clever enough to catch the viewer's attention and, hopefully, give him something to think about for a few miles down the road.

A lot of people ignore the basic rules and try to put too much copy on a board. Or they'll use type that is too small to read. There are plenty of awful boards out there. That's the norm.

The best billboards are the ones that look as if they were easy to do. In reality, however, it usually takes a lot of work to get to that point. You have to be able to hone in on a single idea and get it across in a clever, succinct way. That takes a lot of discipline. But if you can do outdoor well, you can do other advertising well, too.

In the last few years, a lot of talented creative people have realized the potential for doing great work in outdoor. And there's been a surge of exciting work. It's good to see this happening because outdoor has been neglected for a long time.

There are still a lot of creative people who are afraid of outdoor and probably just as many who look down on it because they think it's not as glamorous as magazine or TV advertising. And that's too bad because they're missing a great opportunity.

I've always liked the idea of working with such a huge format. It's kind of like an artist with a giant canvas to work on. It's a lot of work. But it's a lot of fun, too.

Bob Kwait

GOTCHA!

DON'T YOU WISH YOUR ADS STOOD OUT LIKE BALL'S?

THE BALL WCRS PARTNERSHIP

Creative Director
Neil French
Designer
Neil French
Design Agency
The Ball Partnership
Singapore
Writer
Tom Moult
Typographer
Neil French
Client
The Ball Partnership

Creative Director
Kevin Dane O'Callaghan
Designer
Kevin Dane O'Callaghan
Design Agency
Leo Burnett Advertising
Wellington, New Zealand
Writer
Adrian Ogier
Typographer
Artspec Ltd.
Client
Leo Burnett Advertising
Sign
3M New Zealand

OUT TO LAUNCH.

LEO BURNETT *Advertising*

13

TIDY BRITAIN YEAR '90 *Let's do Something!*

Art Director
David Bailey
Design Agency
Broughton-Jacques
Limited
Manchester, England
Photographer
Stephen Ward
Writer
James Denley
Typographer
Typographics 3
Client
The Tidy Britain Group

LITTER. IT'S A RAT'S TALE.
THE ONES WHO DROP IT.

TIDY BRITAIN YEAR '90 *Let's do Something!*

OBVIOUSLY HIS HEAD'S EMPTY TOO.

TIDY BRITAIN YEAR '90 *Let's do Something!*

15

Creative Director
Jac Coverdale
Designer
Jac Coverdale
Design Agency
Clarity Coverdale Rueff
Advertising, Inc.
Minneapolis, U.S.A.
Writer
Joe Alexander
Typographer
Great Faces
Client
MADD (Mothers Against
Drunk Driving)
Sign
Naegele Outdoor
Advertising, Inc.

Art Director
John Littlewood
Designer
Jacqueline Christie
Design Agency
N.W. Ayer
Los Angeles, U.S.A.
Illustrator
Mark Gervase
Writer
Paul Wilcox
Typographer
Andresen
Client
Auto Club of Southern
California
Sign
Patrick Media Group

Creative Directors
Allan Quarry/
William Perry
Design Agency
R.M. Quarry Advertising
Agency Ltd.
Ontario, Canada
Photographer
Fred Hunsberger
Writer
Glen Drummond
Client
The Co-operators
Insurance
Sign
Hook Outdoor
Advertising

Art Director
Michael Price
Designer
Michael Price
Design Agency
Price Leggatt
Advertising/Palmer
Jarvis
Edmonton, Canada
Writer
John Leggatt
Client
Government of Alberta -
Solicitor General
Sign
Hook Outdoor
Advertising

18

Art Director
Bert Gardner
Designer
Jamie Carlson
Design Agency
Bozell Inc.
Minneapolis, U.S.A.
Photographer
Kerry Peterson
Writer
Dick Thomas
Client
United Way

Art Director
Bill Zabowski
Design Agency
Martin/Williams
Advertising
Minneapolis, U.S.A.
Writer
Lyle Wedemeyer
Client
United Way

Art Director
Bert Gardner
Designer
Jamie Carlson
Design Agency
Bozell Inc.
Minneapolis, U.S.A.
Photographer
Rick Dublin
Writers
Dick Briner/Larry Jarvis
Client
Metro 911 Council

19

Creative Director
Rodger Williams
Designer
Rodger Williams
Design Agency
BSB Dorland
London, England
Photographer
Jack Bankhead
Writer
Alan Lofthouse
Typographer
Trevor Slabber
Client
UNICEF

SINCE 1946, WE'VE
BEEN FIGHTING THE
THIRD WORLD WAR.

UNICEF⊛UK
Children count on us. We count on you. Call 01-200 0200.

FOR 3 DAYS THE ONLY
SHOTS IN THE LEBANON
CAME FROM UNICEF.

UNICEF⊛UK Children count on us. We count on you. Call 01-200 0200.

Creative Director
Rodger Williams
Designer
Rodger Williams
Design Agency
BSB Dorland
London, England
Photographer
Jack Bankhead
Writer
Alan Lofthouse
Typographer
Trevor Slabber
Client
UNICEF

Creative Director
Rodger Williams
Designer
Rodger Williams
Design Agency
BSB Dorland
London, England
Photographer
C. Cheetham
Writer
Alan Lofthouse
Typographer
Trevor Slabber
Client
UNICEF

Just think, it could come back as the Wall Street Journal.

No matter how trashy the news, don't ever throw a newspaper in the trash. Recycle instead. To learn more, call the Minneapolis Recycling Program at 348-2917.

Recycle, Minneapolis.

Creative Director
Jac Coverdale
Designer
David Fox
Design Agency
Clarity Coverdale Rueff
Advertising, Inc.
Minneapolis, U.S.A.
Photographer
Mark LaFavor
Writer
Joe Alexander
Typographer
Great Faces
Client
City of Minneapolis,
Recycling Program
Sign
Naegele Outdoor
Advertising, Inc.

This Bud's for us.

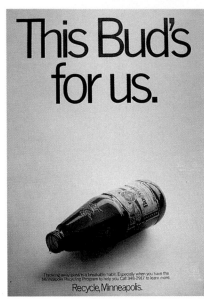

Throwing away glass is a breakable habit. Especially when you have the Minneapolis Recycling Program to help you. Call 348-2917 to learn more.

Recycle, Minneapolis.

Get 10 lives out of a 9 Lives can.

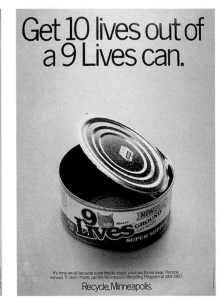

It's time we all became more finicky about what we throw away. Recycle instead. To learn more, call the Minneapolis Recycling Program at 348-2917.

Recycle, Minneapolis.

The only choice of the new generation.

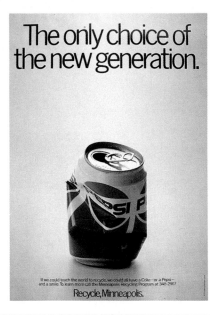

If we could teach the world to recycle, we could all have a Coke—or a Pepsi—and a smile. To learn more call the Minneapolis Recycling Program at 348-2917.

Recycle, Minneapolis.

Finally, proof that reincarnation exists.

Recycle, Minneapolis.

Creative Director
Jac Coverdale
Designer
David Fox
Design Agency
Clarity Coverdale Rueff
Advertising, Inc.
Minneapolis, U.S.A.
Photographer
Mark LaFavor
Writer
Joe Alexander
Typographer
Great Faces
Client
City of Minneapolis
Recycling Program
Sign
Naegele Outdoor
Advertising, Inc.

COMPARED TO THE BUDGETS OF MOST ARMIES, OURS IS A DROP IN THE BUCKET.

THIS ARMY'S BIGGEST BATTLES ARE FOUGHT HERE AT HOME.

Art Director
Bert Gardner
Designers
Craig Tanimoto/
Jamie Carlson
Design Agency
Bozell, Inc.
Minneapolis, U.S.A.
Writer
John Francis
Client
Salvation Army

Art Director
Bert Gardner
Designers
Craig Tanimoto/
Jamie Carlson
Design Agency
Bozell Inc.
Minneapolis, U.S.A.
Writer
John Francis
Client
Salvation Army

Art Director
Bert Gardner
Designers
Craig Tanimoto/
Jamie Carlson
Design Agency
Bozell Inc.
Minneapolis, U.S.A
Photographer
Tom Berthiaume
Writer
John Francis
Client
Salvation Army

Art Director
Bert Gardner
Designer
Larry Jarvis
Design Agency
Bozell Inc.
Minneapolis, U.S.A.
Writer
Glen Wachowiak
Client
Salvation Army

SOME PEOPLE ACTUALLY LOOK FORWARD TO ARMY RATIONS.

2000 YEARS AGO IT TOOK A MIRACLE TO FEED A MULTITUDE.

Helping the hungry takes everyone's support. Please give.

More than 100 years of caring.

IT'S HARD TO BELIEVE IN SANTA WHEN YOU CAN'T IMAGINE YOUR NEXT MEAL.

Our Christmas Food Program is just one way we're helping people this season. Please give.

More than 100 years of caring

HELP WRAP UP A CHILLING SOCIAL PROBLEM.

To help keep Minnesota's needy and homeless children warm this winter, bring your used hats, gloves, mittens and scarves to any Pilgrim or Anderson Cleaners before October 31.

HELP KEEP THE CHILDREN WARM.

UNFORTUNATELY, HE CAN'T BRING THE HOMELESS A PLACE TO LIVE.

Help us provide shelter for thousands of homeless this season. Please give.

More than 100 years of caring

Art Director
Bert Gardner
Designer
Larry Jarvis
Design Agency
Bozell Inc.
Minneapolis, U.S.A.
Writer
Glen Wachowiak
Client
Salvation Army

Art Director
Bert Gardner
Designer
Mike Murray
Design Agency
Bozell Inc.
Minneapolis, U.S.A.
Writer
John Francis
Client
Salvation Army

Art Director
Bert Gardner
Designer
Larry Jarvis
Design Agency
Bozell Inc.
Minneapolis, U.S.A.
Writer
Glen Wachowiak
Client
Salvation Army

Art Director
Bert Gardner
Designers
Craig Tanimoto/
Jamie Carlson
Design Agency
Bozell Inc.
Minneapolis, U.S.A .
Photographer
Tom Berthiaume
Writer
John Francis
Client
Salvation Army

Art Director
Wally Krysciak
Design Agency
McKim Advertising
Toronto, Canada
Photographer
Y.W. Lung
Writer
Catherine Nolan
Typographer
Composing Room/
Cooper & Beatty
Client
The Salvation Army
Sign
H.S.P. Graphics/
Mediacom Inc.

THE SALVATION ARMY

God knows you can make a difference

NOT ALL ARMIES PUNISH DESERTION.

Art Directors
Mark Flett/Adam Regan
Designer
Adam Regan
Design Agency
Golley Slater & Partners
London, England
Photographer
Gary Redmore
Writers
Malachy Quinn/Alison
King/Adam Regan
Typographers
Mike Rix/Adam Regan
Client
The Blue Cross

THE BLUE CROSS NEEDS YOU.

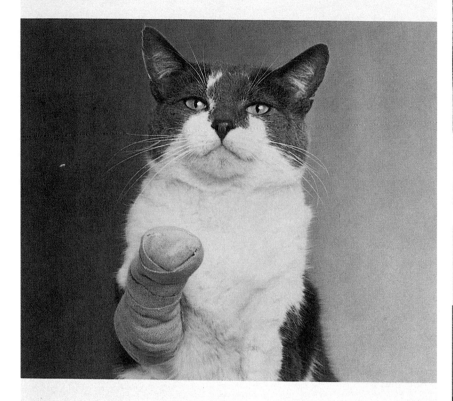

Every year The Blue Cross hospitals see thousands of pets whose owners cannot afford vet fees. They also take in sick and injured strays. Please help the work go on.

BLUE✚CROSS
ANIMAL WELFARE SOCIETY

The Blue Cross relies solely on donations: The Blue Cross Animals Hospital, 1 Hugh St, Victoria, London SW1V 1QQ. Registered Charity No 224392. Telephone 01-834 5556.

WE HAVE TO STRETCH FURTHER.

From stray kittens to retired horses. From sick puppies to lost parakeets to injured rabbits, no needy animal is turned away from our door.

BLUE✚CROSS
ANIMAL WELFARE SOCIETY

The Blue Cross relies solely on donations: The Blue Cross Animals Hospital, 1 Hugh St, Victoria, London SW1V 1QQ. Registered Charity No 224392. Telephone 01-834 5556.

WHAT KIND OF WORM COULD BLIND A CHILD?

A worm found in dog's excrement. Yet regular worming not only controls it but also improves the health of your dog. Worming costs very little. Surely a child's sight is worth it.

BLUE✚CROSS
ANIMAL WELFARE SOCIETY

The Blue Cross relies solely on donations: The Blue Cross Animals Hospital, 1 Hugh St, Victoria, London SW1V 1QQ. Registered Charity No 224392. Telephone 01-834 5556.

STOP THIS ELDERLY COUPLE BEING SPLIT UP.

Alice only had Patch. Patch only had Alice. And the only thing that threatened to come between them was vet fees, which Alice simply couldn't afford. Fortunately she was able to come to The Blue Cross Animals Hospital.

BLUE✚CROSS
ANIMAL WELFARE SOCIETY

The Blue Cross relies solely on donations: The Blue Cross Animals Hospital, 1 Hugh St, Victoria, London SW1V 1QQ. Registered Charity No 224392. Telephone 01-834 5556.

ATTRACTIVE YOUNG LADIES LOOKING FOR LIFELONG COMPANIONS.

Intelligent. Playful. Interested in a permanent loving relationship. And looking for a good home. Just three of thousands of homeless pets that turn up on The Blue Cross's doorstep every year.

BLUE✚CROSS
ANIMAL WELFARE SOCIETY

The Blue Cross relies solely on donations: The Blue Cross Animals Hospital, 1 Hugh St, Victoria, London SW1V 1QQ. Registered Charity No 224392. Telephone 01-834 5556.

Design Agency
Cassidy Foundation
Los Angeles, U.S.A.
Client
Cassidy Foundation
Sign
Patrick Media Group

Art Director
Bob Kwait
Designer
Bob Kwait
Design Agency
Phillips-Ramsey
San Diego, U.S.A.
Photographer
Chris Wimpey
Writer
Joe Lazo
Typographer
Laurie Dotson
Client
The Foundation for Family
Literacy

Art Director
Gus Pitsikoulis
Designer
Gus Pitsikoulis
Design Agency
Babbit & Reiman
Advertising
Atlanta, U.S.A.
Writer
Joey Reiman
Typographer
Characters
Client
Atlanta Jewish Federation
Sign
Adams Outdoor

Art Director
Sharon Low
Designer
Sharon Low
Design Agency
Ackerley
Communications of the
Northwest
Seattle, U.S.A.
Illustrator
Sharon Low
Client
Piper Creek Watershed
Sign
Ackerley
Communications of the
Northwest

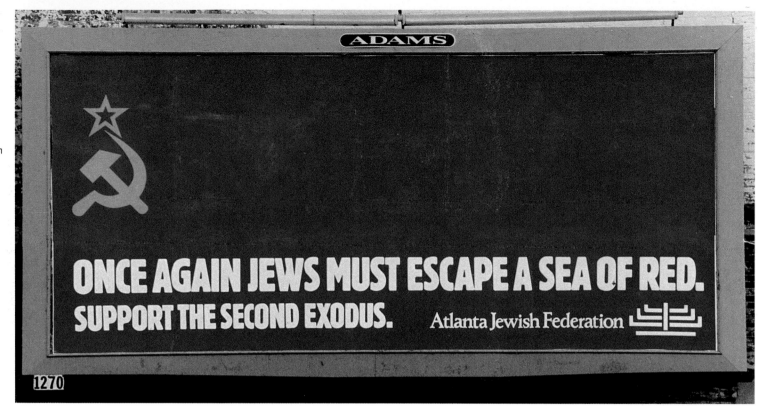

Can anyone make sense of it?

Can anyone make sense of it?

Art Director
Peter Ibbitson
Design Agency
FCB (Advertising) Limited
London, England
Writer
Eddie Haydock
Typographers
Mitchell Gumbley/
Steve Ronchetti
Client
Billy Graham Mission '89

Made sense of it yet?

Come and hear one man who can make sense of it. Billy Graham.
—— Upton Park: 14-16 JUNE · Crystal Palace: 21-23 JUNE · Earls Court: 26 JUNE -1 JULY——

Art Director
Bert Gardner
Designer
Chris Lincoln
Design Agency
Bozell Inc.
Minneapolis, U.S.A.
Photographer
Rick Dublin
Writer
Dick Thomas
Client
Mn. Dept. of Public
Safety/Mn. Inst. of Public
Health

Art Director
Mary Sherbowich
Designer
Brian Skinner
Design Agency
Campbell & Michener
Toronto, Canada
Photographer/Illustrator
Tom White
Typographer
Word For Word
Client
Scouts Toronto
Sign
Mediacom Inc.

30

Art Director
Wendy Hansen
Photographer
Rick Dublin
Design Agency
Martin/Williams
Advertising
Minneapolis, U.S.A.
Writer
Lyle Wedemeyer
Client
MN Department of Health

Art Director
Daniel Martinez
Design Agency
Patrick Media Group
Los Angeles, U.S.A.
Writer
Daniel Martinez
Client
Art Bulletin Competition
Sign
Patrick Media Group

Art Director
May Sun
Design Agency
Patrick Media Group
Los Angeles, U.S.A
Writer
May Sun
Client
Art Bulletin Competition
Sign
Patrick Media Group

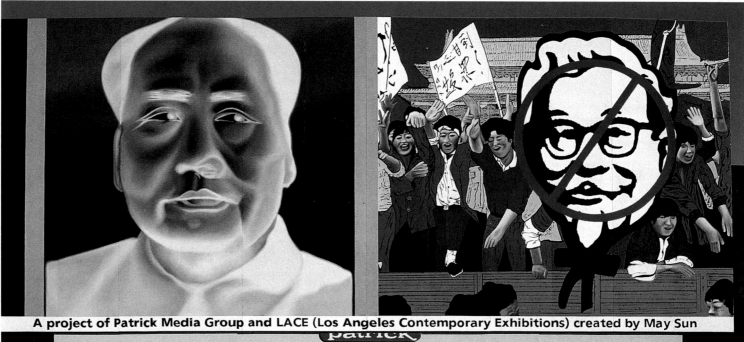

DON'T HATE ME BECAUSE I'M BEAUTIFUL ...

A project of Patrick Media Group and LACE (Los Angeles Contemporary Exhibitions) created by Elizabeth Garrison & Victor Henderson

A project of Patrick Media Group and LACE (Los Angeles Contemporary Exhibitions) created by Hilja Keading

Art Directors
Victor Henderson/
Elizabeth Garrison
Design Agency
Patrick Media Group
Los Angeles, U.S.A.
Writers
Victor Henderson/
Elizabeth Garrison
Client
Art Bulletin Competition
Sign
Patrick Media Group

Art Director
Hilja Keading
Design Agency
Patrick Media Group
Los Angeles, U.S.A.
Writer
Hilja Keading
Client
Art Bulletin Competition
Sign
Patrick Media Group

Art Director
Phil Soreide
Designer
Don Personius
Design Agency
Ripley-Woodbury
Advertising, Inc.
Cerritos, U.S.A.
Client
Downey Community
Hospital
Sign
Patrick Media Group/
Robert Keith & Co. Inc.

Art Director
Martin P. O'Neill
Designer
Martin P. O'Neill
Design Agency
Innes & Willett
Advertising
Baltimore, U.S.A.
Writer
Jack Willett III
Client
Baltimore's Children's
Hospital
Sign
Penn Advertising

Art Director
James Wang
Design Agency
Chuck Ruhr Advertising
Minneapolis, U.S.A.
Writer
Bill Johnson
Client
United Hospital

Art Director
Vivian Ducas
Designer
Vivian Ducas
Design Agency
Ogilvy & Mather
New York, U.S.A.
Illustrator
Steven Guarnaccia
Client
A.E. Lepage Realty
Company

Art Directors
Constance Beck/
Terry P. Graboski
Designers
Constance Beck/
Terry P. Graboski
Design Agency
Beck & Graboski Design
Office
Santa Monica, U.S.A.
Typographer
Adcompositors Inc.
Client
IDM Development Corp.
Sign
Coast Signs

Art Directors
Terry P. Graboski/
Constance Beck
Designers
Terry P. Graboski/
Constance Beck
Design Agency
Beck & Graboski Design
Office
Santa Monica, U.S.A.
Typographer
Adcompositors Inc.
Client
IDM Development Corp.
Sign
Bob Machan Signs

TWO IMPORTANT POINTS WHEN BUYING A HOME

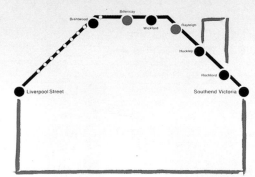

LOCATION AND LOCATION

Magnolias
G R E A T B U R S T E A D
4 BEDROOM DETACHED HOMES

Get your travelling day off to a better start with a new home at Great Burstead, near Billericay, or Dene Gardens, Rayleigh. You'll find a choice of superb family homes on two exclusive developments convenient for the Liverpool Street line.

Dene Gardens
R A Y L E I G H

Visit a Lovell Home this weekend and we'll tell you about helpful schemes like Part Exchange or Equity Share that can be tailored to your circumstances. With our new optional Homestyle package, you can create your perfect interior, with a choice of quality carpets, curtains and fabrics selected by a leading designer.

For further information please ring (0268) 741111

Lovell Homes
We're different. We think.

Lovell Homes Eastern Ltd., Lovell House, Castle Road, Rayleigh, Essex SS6 7RR. Telephone :(0268) 741111

IS THE OLD HOME GETTING YOU DOWN?

Magnolias
G R E A T B U R S T E A D
4 BEDROOM DETACHED HOMES

Blow away the cobwebs and step into a brand new four-bedroom detached house with a superb specification. You'll no longer be haunted by the repairs and decorating that never go away. Move into a light, airy home that gets your travelling day off to a better start on an exclusive development convenient for the Liverpool Street line.

Visit a Lovell Home this weekend and we'll tell you about helpful schemes like Part Exchange or Equity Share that can be tailored to your circumstances. With our new optional Homestyle package, you can create your perfect interior, with a choice of quality carpets, curtains and fabrics selected by a leading designer. Truly a home to lift your spirits.

For further information please ring (0268) 741111

Lovell Homes
We're different. We think.

Lovell Homes Eastern Ltd., Lovell House, Castle Road, Rayleigh, Essex SS6 7RR. Telephone :(0268) 741111

YES DARLING, SIMPLY EVERYONE'S MOVING TO CONYERS PLACE

Conyers Place
N r . B U R Y S T . E D M U N D S
4/5 BEDROOM DETACHED HOMES

You can still get a home in the country. Family homes on large plots up to ¼ acre with outstanding exterior features such as flint fascias in a village environment. The specification is superb, including entry phone security system, audio system with outlets in selected rooms, and a quality conservatory. We've combined the traditional values of country life in a home that represents the best in contemporary design and specification.

With our optional Homestyle service you can create your perfect interior - discussing your choice of carpets, curtains and fabrics with our consultant designer. If you want the best out of life, come to Conyers Place showhome and start planning your home in the country. Anything else simply isn't Conyers.

For further information please ring (0284) 878206

Lovell Homes
We're different. We think.

Lovell Homes Eastern Ltd., Lovell House, Castle Road, Rayleigh, Essex SS6 7RR. Telephone :(0268) 741111

Art Director
Ian Wilson
Designer
Yvonne Booth
Design Agency
Facet Group
Essex, England
Writer
Ian Linton
Typographer
Facet
Client
Lovell Homes

36

HE CAN'T WAIT TO GET BACK TO A LOVELL HOME

Regis Park
SITTINGBOURNE

4 BEDROOM DETACHED HOMES

At the end of the working day, wouldn't it be good to come back to a Lovell Home. Just a few minutes from the main line station, you'll find a choice of superb family homes on an exclusive development at Regis Park.

Visit a Lovell Home this weekend and we'll tell you about helpful schemes like Part Exchange or Equity Share that can be tailored to your circumstances. With our new optional Homestyle package, you can create your perfect interior, with a choice of quality carpets, curtains and fabrics selected by a leading designer. Hurry, don't get caught in the rush.

For further information please ring (0795) 479137

Lovell Homes

Lovell Homes Eastern Ltd., Lovell House, Castle Road, Rayleigh, Essex SS6 7RR. Telephone: (0268) 741111

TIME IS ON YOUR SIDE WHEN YOU BUY A LOVELL HOME.

Dene Gardens
RAYLEIGH

4 BEDROOM DETACHED HOMES

If you're fed up with clock watching, it's time you got to grips with the daily journey by moving to a new Lovell Home just a few minutes from the main line station. You'll find a choice of superb family homes on an exclusive development at Dene Gardens.

Visit a Lovell Home this weekend and we'll tell you about helpful schemes like Part Exchange or Equity Share that can be tailored to your circumstances. With our new optional Homestyle package, you can create your perfect interior, with a choice of quality carpets, curtains and fabrics selected by a leading designer. You'll have the time of your life in a Lovell Home. **For further information please ring (0268) 741111**

Lovell Homes

Lovell Homes Eastern Ltd., Lovell House, Castle Road, Rayleigh, Essex SS6 7RR. Telephone: (0268) 741111

Art Director
Jeff Jackson
Designer
Jeff Jackson
Design Agency
Reed Ham Jackson, Inc.
San Antonio, U.S.A.
Illustrator
Robert Cardellino
Writer
David Ham
Typographer
Rose Marie Reyna
Client
Sitterle Homes
Sign
Rollins Outdoor

AIRPORTS HAVE ALWAYS BEEN A GREAT PLACE TO SPREAD YOUR MESSAGE.

Place your ad here and you could attract quite a following. Call 726-5355.

· AIRPORT MEDIA MARKETING ·

Unlike your luggage, your message won't get lost here.

Place your ad here and the only thing you'll stand to lose is your competition. Call 726-5355.

AIRPORT MEDIA MARKETING

People actually travel great distances to read our ads.

If you're trying to reach people who are going places, place your ad here. Call 726-5355.

AIRPORT MEDIA MARKETING

made you look! made you look!

Even a child could see that airport advertising works. Call 726-5355.

AIRPORT MEDIA MARKETING

Art Director
Pam Conboy Mariutto
Design Agency
Martin/Williams
Advertising
Minneapolis, U.S.A.
Writer
Tom Leydon
Client
Naegele Outdoor
Sign
Naegele Outdoor
Advertising, Inc.

Art Director
Jeff Jackson
Designers
Jeff Jackson/David Ham
Design Agency
Reed Ham Jackson, Inc.
San Antonio, U.S.A.
Writer
David Ham
Client
Rollins Outdoor
Advertising/Reed Ham
Jackson, Inc.
Sign
SA Foam Fabricators

Art Director
Dennis Bruce
Designer
Tony Kerr
Design Agency
Miller Myers Bruce
DallaCosta
Toronto, Canada
Photographer
Deborah Samuels
Writer
Bruce MacDonald
Typographer
Techni Process Lettering
Ltd.
Client
Mediacom Inc.
Sign
Mediacom Inc.

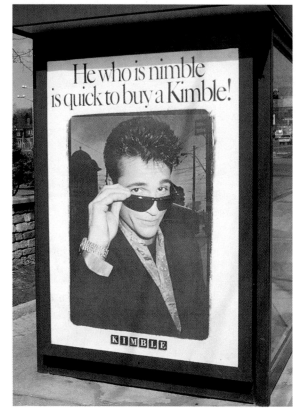

40

Creative Director
Peter Angelos
Art Director
Larry Corby
Design Agency
Foote, Cone & Belding
Los Angeles, U.S.A.
Writer
Peter Angelos
Typographer
Andresen
Client
U.S. Forest Service
Sign
Patrick Media Group/
Myer

Creative Director
Jac Coverdale
Designer
Craig Tanimoto
Design Agency
Clarity Coverdale Rueff
Advertising, Inc.
Minneapolis, U.S.A.
Photographer
Allen Mathewitz
Writer
Joe Alexander
Typographer
Great Faces
Client
Minneapolis Metropolitan
YMCA
Sign
Naegele Outdoor
Advertising, Inc.

Art Directors
Dave Kelso/Robert Ito
Designer
Robert Ito
Design Agency
J. Walter Thompson
Toronto, Canada
Photographer
Richard Picton
Writer
Steve Roxborough
Typographer
Eklipse
Client
Warner Lambert
Sign
Mediacom Inc.

Art Director
Gray Abraham
Designer
Gray Abraham
Design Agency
J. Walter Thompson
Toronto, Canada
Illustrator
Spitting Image
Writer
John George
Typographer
Spitting Image
Client
Warner Lambert -
Chiclets
Sign
Bomac

43

Deux façons d'être sûr de votre haleine le matin.

Le nouveau Clorets

Êtes-vous à l'abri de la mauvaise haleine?

Clorets, c'est plus que du bonbon.

Êtes-vous à l'abri de la mauvaise haleine?

Clorets, c'est plus que du bonbon.

Êtes-vous à l'abri de la mauvaise haleine?

Clorets, c'est plus que du bonbon.

If you think you might have bad breath, don't say anything.

Be sure about your breath. Use Clorets.

Art Directors
François Larocque/
Guy Simard
Designer
François Larocque
Design Agency
J. Walter Thompson
Montréal, Canada
Photographer
Jean Vachon
Writer
Martin Gosslin
Client
Warner Lambert
Sign
Mediacom Inc.

Art Directors
Marlene Hore/
Stephanie Richmond
Designer
Stephanie Richmond
Design Agency
J. Walter Thompson
Toronto, Canada
Writer
John George
Typographer
Type Studio
Client
Warner Lambert
Sign
Mediacom Inc.

Art Directors
François Larocque/
Guy Simard
Designer
François Larocque
Design Agency
J. Walter Thompson
Montréal, Canada
Illustrator
Alain Massicotte
Writer
Martin Gosslin
Client
Warner Lambert
Sign
Mediacom Inc.

THE BURGERVILLE COLOSSAL, SLIGHTLY ENLARGED.

BurgerVille USA

Creative Director
Bill Borders
Art Director
Tom Kelly
Designer
Tom Kelly
Design Agency
Borders Perrin &
Norrander
Portland, U.S.A.
Photographer
Pete Stone
Writer
Bill Borders
Typographer
BP&N Typesetting
Client
Burgerville, USA

Creative Director
Alan Russell
Art Director
Tony Woods
Design Agency
Palmer Jarvis
Vancouver, Canada
Photographer
Hans Sipma
Client
Canada Safeway
Sign
Gallop+Gallop

Creative Director
Peter Angelos
Art Director
Larry Corby
Design Agency
Foote, Cone & Belding
Los Angeles, U.S.A.
Photographer
Patrice Migneaux
Writer
Peter Angelos
Typographer
Andresen
Client
Sunkist Growers, Inc.
Sign
Patrick Media Group/
Myer Showprint

Creative Director
Mike Wagman
Art Director
Ann King
Design Agency
Foote, Cone & Belding
Los Angeles, U.S.A.
Photographer
Patrice Migneaux
Writer
Ann King
Typographer
Andresen
Client
Sunkist Growers, Inc.
Sign
Patrick Media Group/
Myer Showprint

Creative Director
Dave Tyree
Art Director
Chris Chaffin
Design Agency
Ketchum Advertising
San Francisco, U.S.A.
Photographer
Diane Padys
Writer
Mickey Lonchar
Typographer
Ketchum Productions
Client
Safeway Inc.
Sign
Patrick Media Group

Red and white for the winter blues.

MEDIACOM

GOODNESS
Stouffer's Macaroni and Cheese
Only the best. Stouffer's.

MEDIACOM

NEW Instant OXO
15 Chicken Bouillon PACKETS
OXO

FROM ZERO
TO CHICKEN SOUP
IN 2.8 SECONDS.

NEW INSTANT
OXO FLAVOUR PACKETS.

Creative Director
Mike Wagman
Art Director/Designer
Larry Corby
Design Agency
Foote, Cone & Belding
Los Angeles, U.S.A.
Photographer
Patrice Migneaux
Writer
Jack Foster
Typographer
Andresen
Client
The California Milk
Advisory Board
Sign
Patrick Media Group/
Horn

Art Director
Caroline Jarvis
Designer
Carolin Jarvis
Design Agency
BCP Strategie
Montréal, Canada
Photographer
P. Baumgartner
Writer
Jean Gamache
Typographer
M & H Typography
Client
Yoplait
Sign
Mediacom Inc.

Art Director
Susan Butterworth
Designer
Susan Butterworth
Design Agency
Daily & Associates
Los Angeles, U.S.A.
Photographer
Dan Wolfe
Writer
Claudia Caplan
Typographer
Andresen
Client
Carnation Ice Cream
Sign
Patrick Media Group

Art Director
Mary McInerny
Designer
Mary McInerny
Design Agency
Grey Advertising, Inc.
Los Angeles, U.S.A.
Illustrator
Patrice Migneaux
Writer
Kathy Grossman
Typographer
Characters and Color
Client
Knudsen/Kraft
Sign
Patrick Media Group

Art Director
Sally Wagner
Designer
Sally Wagner
Design Agency
Martin/Williams
Advertising, Inc.
Minneapolis, U.S.A.
Illustrator
Kent Severson
Writer
Emily Scott
Typographer
Great Faces
Client
Baker's Square
Sign
Whipson Poster/Patrick
Media Group

Art Directors
Terry Tomalty/
Leah Curley
Designer
Terry Tomalty
Design Agency
J. Walter Thompson
Montréal, Canada
Illustrator
Roger Hill
Writer
Leah Curley
Client
Kraft General Foods Inc.
Sign
Mediacom Inc.

Art Directors
René-Michel Vachon/
Guy Simard
Designer
René-Michel Vachon
Design Agency
J. Walter Thompson
Montréal, Canada
Photographer
Tilt Inc.
Writer
Michel Bergeron
Client
Kellogg's
Sign
Mediacom Inc.

Art Directors
Terry Tomalty/
Leah Curley
Designer
Terry Tomalty
Design Agency
J. Walter Thompson
Montréal, Canada
Illustrator
Roger Hill
Writer
Leah Curley
Client
Kraft General Foods Inc.
Sign
Mediacom Inc.

Creative Director
Rick Davis
Art Director
Ken Boyd
Designer
Ken Boyd
Design Agency
Young & Rubicam
Toronto, Canada
Photographer
Stanley Wong
Writer
Rick Davis
Typographer
Hunter Brown
Client
Kodak Canada Inc.
Sign
Hook Outdoor
Advertising

55

Art Director
Sue Solie
Designers
Linda Kaplan/
Nick Gisonde
Design Agency
J. Walter Thompson
New York, U.S.A.
Photographer
Barbara Campbell
Writer
Mary Warner
Client
Eastman Kodak
Sign
Patrick Media Group

Art Directors
Gordon Melcher/
Ed Segura/
Kyle Lewis
Design Agency
Robert Elen & Associates
Los Angeles, U.S.A.
Writers
Robert Elen/
Brian Gross
Client
Zenith

Art Director
Leif Nielsen
Design Agency
Carder Gray DDB
Needham
Toronto, Canada
Illustrator
Theo Dimson
Writer
Steve Conover
Typographer
Hunter Brown Ltd.
Client
Parfumerie Versailles
Ltee.
Sign
Mediacom Inc.

Art Director
René Larivière
Designers
Patrick Brodeur/
André Dubois/
Steeve Gagnon
Design Agency
Marketel Publim Inc.
Québec, Canada
Illustrator
André Dubois
Writer
Luc Saint-Hilaire
Typographer
Caractéra
Client
Elite portes et fenêtres
Sign
Mediacom Inc.

Art Director
Roger Gingras
Designers
Roger Gingras/
Luc Saint-Hilaire
Design Agency
Marketel Publim Inc.
Québec, Canada
Illustrator
André Dubois
Writer
Luc Saint-Hilaire
Typographer
Caractéra
Client
Elite portes et fenêtres
Sign
Mediacom Inc.

Plus de 400 autres modèles en magasin. **LA FOIRE DU VENTILATEUR**

Art Director
Leon Berger
Designer
Roger Gariépy
Design Agency
Young & Rubicam
Montréal, Canada
Illustrator
Helmut Lungader
Writer
André Paradis
Typographer
M & H
Client
La Foire du Ventilateur
Sign
Mediacom Inc.

Creative Director
Rick Davis
Art Director
Leif Nielsen
Designer
Leif Nielsen
Design Agency
Young & Rubicam
Toronto, Canada
Illustrator
Desmond Montique
Writer
Steve Conover
Typographer
Hunter Brown
Client
Binney & Smith

Art Director
Julia Koo
Design Agency
Grey Advertising
Vancouver, Canada
Illustrator
Ken Koo Creative
Writer
Mark Levine
Typographer
Grey Advertising
Client
General Paint
Sign
Hook Outdoor
Advertising

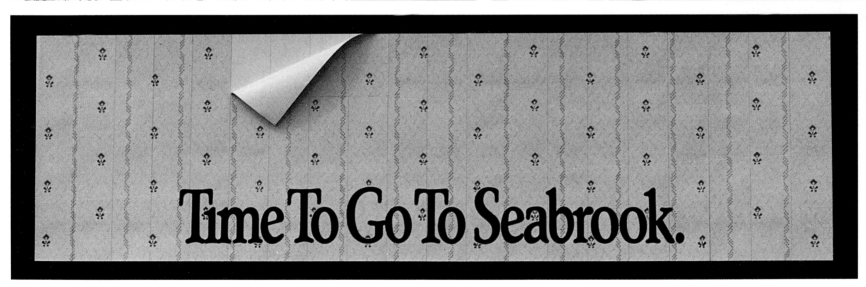

Creative Director
Michael H. Thompson
Art Director
Trace Hallowell
Design Agency
Thompson & Company,
Memphis, U.S.A.
Writer
Trace Hallowell
Typographer
Great Faces
Client
Seabrook Wallcoverings,
Inc.
Sign
Naegele Outdoor
Advertising, Inc.

Art Director
Jeff Layton
Designer
Jeff Layton
Design Agency
Jeff Layton & Assoc. Ltd./
Grey Canada
Toronto, Canada
Illustrator
Terry Puplett/
Sharpshooter
Productions
Writer
Jim Catlin
Typographer
Typsettra
Client
Airwick Canada
Sign
H&S Reliance/Trans Ad

Bad breath can be positively frightful.

Fortunately, fresh breath is a spray away.

Bad breath can be an enormous problem.

Fortunately, fresh breath is a spray away.

Bad breath can kill an evening.

Fortunately, fresh breath is a spray away.

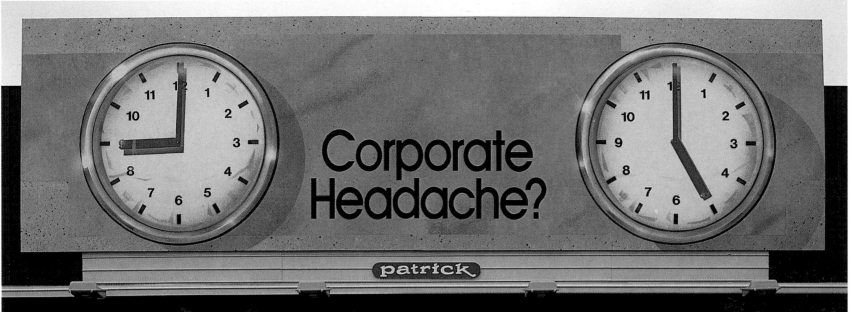

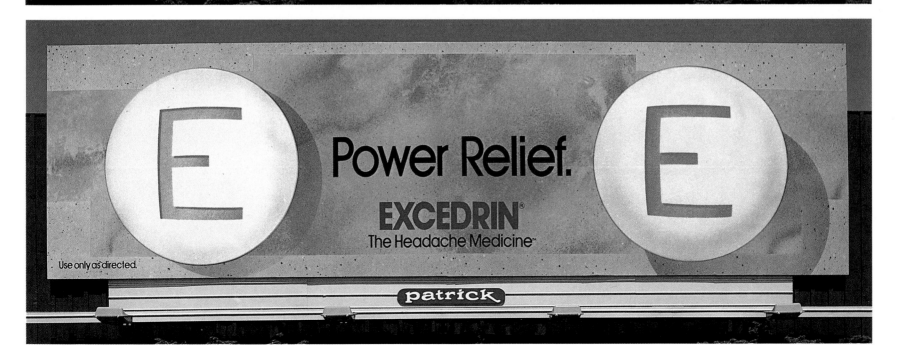

Creative Director
Jane Talcott
Art Director
Dave Rauch
Designer
Dave Rauch
Design Agency
DDB Needham
Worldwide
New York, U.S.A.
Illustrator
Joel Nakamura
Writer
Dan Brooks
Typographer
Printgraphics
Client
Bristol-Myers Squibb Co.
Sign
Patrick Media Group

63

Art Director
Gus Pitsikoulis
Designer
Brad Ramsey
Design Agency
Babbit & Reiman
Advertising
Atlanta, U.S.A.
Photographer
(Stock)
Writer
David Rudinsky
Typographer
Characters
Client
Eye Associates
Sign
3M Outdoor

Art Director
Gus Pitsikoulis
Designer
Gus Pitsikoulis
Design Agency
Babbit & Reiman
Advertising
Atlanta, U.S.A.
Photographer
Roger Bacuch
Writer
Ralph McGill Jr.
Typographer
Characters
Client
Noelle Day Spa
Sign
Adams Outdoor

Loyal & Hearty.

Helping pets live
longer, healthier lives™
® © Ralston Purina Company, 1987

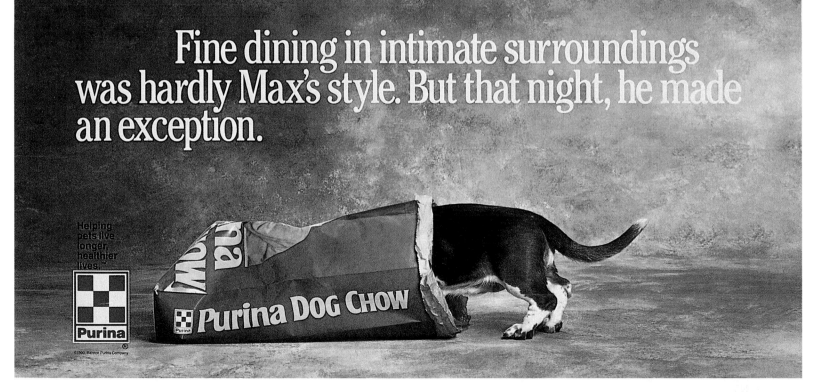

Fine dining in intimate surroundings was hardly Max's style. But that night, he made an exception.

Helping
pets live
longer,
healthier
lives.

Purina DOG CHOW

Art Director
Gail Donnelly
Design Agency
Centra Advertising
Company
St. Louis, U.S.A.
Photographer
Eileen Glenn Studio
Client
Ralston Purina Company

Art Director
Tim Cenova
Design Agency
Centra Advertising
Company
St. Louis, U.S.A.
Photographer
Jean Moss
Writer
Susan McMichael
Client
Purina Dog Chow

Art Director
Marcee Ruby
Designer
Marcee Ruby
Design Agency
J. Walter Thompson
Toronto, Canada
Illustrator
Bob Fortier
Writer
Shelley Ambrose
Typographer
Bob Fortier
Client
Warner Lambert - Adams
Brands
Sign
H.S.P. Graphics

67

Art Directors
Howard Alstad/
Allan Kazmer
Design Agency
Carder Gray DDB
Needham
Toronto, Canada
Illustrator
Paula Munck
Writer
Philippe Garneau
Typographer
Bomac
Client
Merrell Dow
Pharmaceuticals Inc.
Sign
Mediacom Inc.

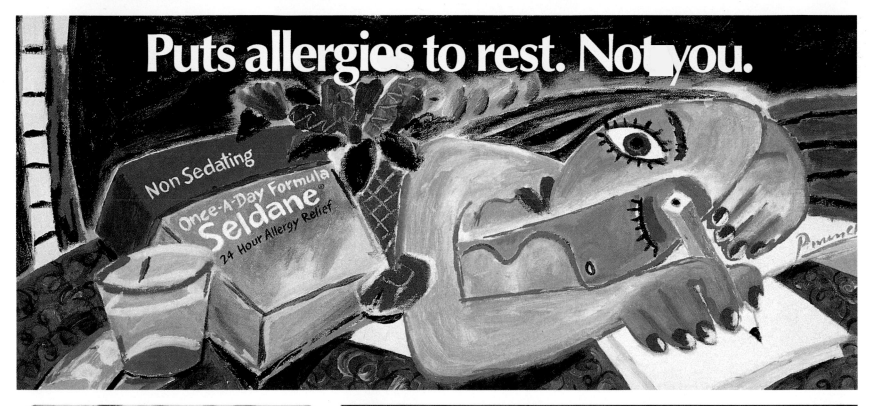

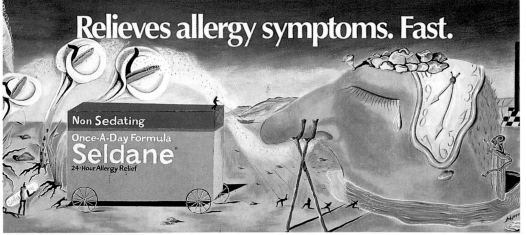

The Only Thing In Your House That Has A More Lifelike Picture Than A Toshiba Television.

Art Director
Peter Barron
Designer
Peter Barron
Design Agency
J. Walter Thompson
Toronto, Canada
Photographer
Bill McLeod
Writers
Peter Barron/Avrom Volt
Typographer
Typsettra
Client
Toshiba
Sign
Mediacom Inc.

TOSHIBA

The Only Thing In Your Living Room That's Easier To Operate Than A Toshiba VCR.

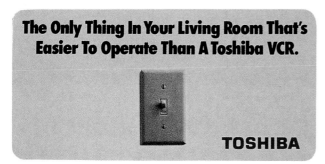

TOSHIBA

The Only Thing In Your House That Does More For Your Ears Than A Toshiba Stereo.

TOSHIBA

The Only Thing In Your Kitchen That's More Durable Than A Toshiba Microwave.

TOSHIBA

Creative Director
Pierre Audet
Art Director
Pierre Drouin
Design Agency
Foug
Montréal, Canada
Photographer
Monic Richard
Writers
Michel Lopez/
Dianna Carr
Typographer
Foug
Client
Raymond Lanctôt/
Vuarnet
Sign
Repro 2000/
H.S.P./
Hook Outdoor
Advertising

Creative Director
Pierre Audet
Art Director
Pierre Drouin
Design Agency
Foug
Montréal, Canada
Photographer
Monic Richard
Writers
Michel Lopez/
Dianna Carr
Typographer
Foug
Client
Raymond Lanctôt/
Vuarnet
Sign
Le Groupe C.I.G./
Mediacom Inc./
Hook Outdoor
Advertising

Creative Director
Pierre Audet
Art Director
Pierre Drouin
Design Agency
Foug
Montréal, Canada
Photographer
Monic Richard
Writers
Michel Lopez/
Dianna Carr
Typographer
Foug
Client
Raymond Lanctôt/TCHAK
Sign
Le Groupe C.I.G./
H.S.P./Hook Outdoor
Advertising

Art Director
Brian Harrod
Design Agency
Harrod & Mirlin
Toronto, Canada
Photographer
Bert Bell
Writer
Ian Mirlin
Typographer
Words
Client
Levi Strauss
Sign
Mediacom Inc.

Creative Directors
Brian Harrod/Ian Mirlin
Art Director
Dianne Eastman
Design Agency
Harrod & Mirlin
Toronto, Canada
Photographer
Bert Bell
Writer
Bill Daniel
Typographer
Words
Client
Levi Strauss
Sign
Mediacom Inc.

Art Director
James Jung
Design Agency
Harrod & Mirlin
Toronto, Canada
Photographer
Bert Bell
Writer
Brian Harrod
Client
Bern Gorecki/Levi Strauss
& Co. (Canada) Inc.
Sign
Mediacom Inc.

Art Director
Derek Chapman
Designer
Derek Chapman
Design Agency
J. Walter Thompson
Toronto, Canada
Photographer
Terry Collier
Writers
Derek Chapman/
Jeff Butler
Typographer
Hunter Brown
Client
G.W.G.
Sign
HSP Graphics/
Mediacom Inc.

Art Director
Rob Richards
Designer
Rob Richards
Design Agency
Gannett Outdoor of
Arizona
Phoenix, U.S.A.
Client
Custom Shirt Co.
Sign
Gannett Outdoor of
Arizona

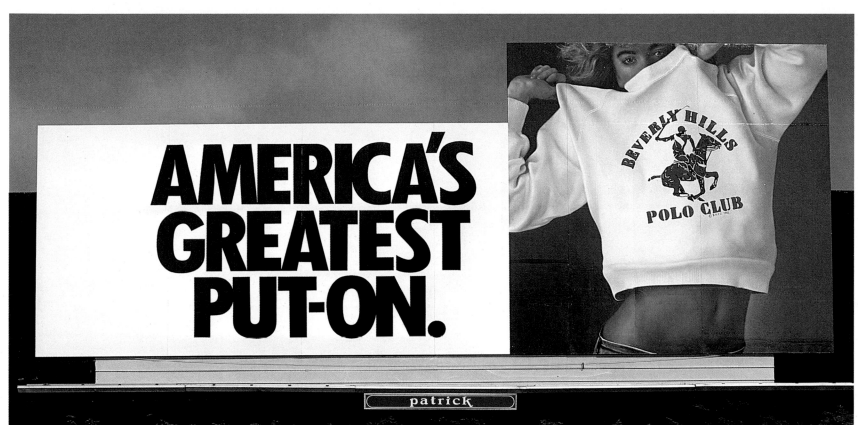

Art Director
Israel Leibowitz
Design Agency
Israel Leibowitz
Los Angeles, U.S.A.
Client
Beverly Hills Polo Club
Sign
Patrick Media Group

Art Director
Nicole Fréchette
Designer
René-Michel Vachon
Design Agency
Publicité Martin inc.
Montréal, Canada
Photographer
Sylvain Côté
Writer
Nicole Fréchette
Typographer
Avant-Garde
Client
Sogides
Sign
Mediacom Inc.

Art Director
Rick Rietveld
Designer
Rick Rietveld
Design Agency
Maui and Sons
Costa Mesa, U.S.A.
Illustrator
Rick Rietveld
Writer
Rick Rietveld
Typographer
Alphabet Type
Client
Maui and Sons
Sign
Patrick Media Group

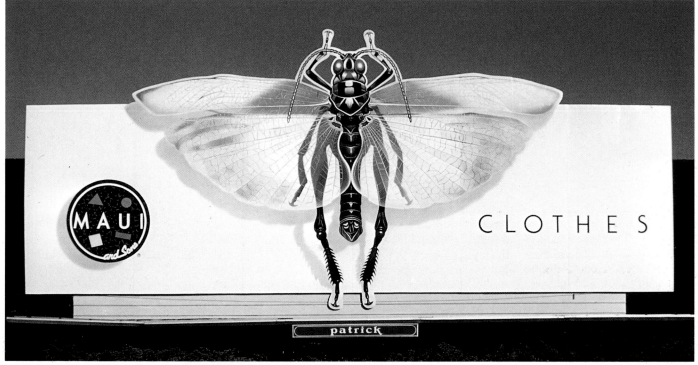

Art Director
Paul Hains
Designer
Paul Hains
Design Agency
Bozell Palmer Bonner
Toronto, Canada
Photographer
Rino Noto
Writer
Paul Hains
Client
Harvey Woods
Underwear
Sign
Mediacom Inc.

Art Director
Clodagh Wheatley
Designer
Clodagh Wheatley
Design Agency
Wheatley & Rosenberg
Montréal, Canada
Illustrator
Pamela Quinn
Client
ALDO SHOES
Sign
Urbanoscope

Creative Director
Bill Borders
Art Director
Tom Kelly
Designer
Tom Kelly
Design Agency
Borders Perrin &
Norrander
Portland, U.S.A.
Illustrator
Pete Stone
Writer
Bill Borders
Typographer
BP&N Typesetting
Client
AVIA Athletic Footwear

Art Director
Michael Pnieuf
Designer
Michael Pnieuf
Design Agency
Wieden & Kennedy
Portland, U.S.A.
Illustrator
Pete Stone
Writer
Jim Niswold
Client
Nike, Inc.
Sign
Patrick Media Group

Art Director
Peter Moore
Designer
Peter Moore
Client
Nike, Inc.
Sign
Patrick Media Group

Art Director
Pamela Clinkard
Design Agency
BBDO
New York, U.S.A.
Illustrator
Eric Meola
Client
Pepsi-Cola Co.
Sign
Patrick Media Group

Creative Director
Neil McGregor
Art Director
Claude Brie
Designer
Claude Brie
Design Agency
MacLaren:Lintas
Advertising
Montréal, Canada
Photographer
Carl Valiquet
Writer
Richard Desautels
Client
Molson/Laurentide
Sign
P.O.S. Inc.

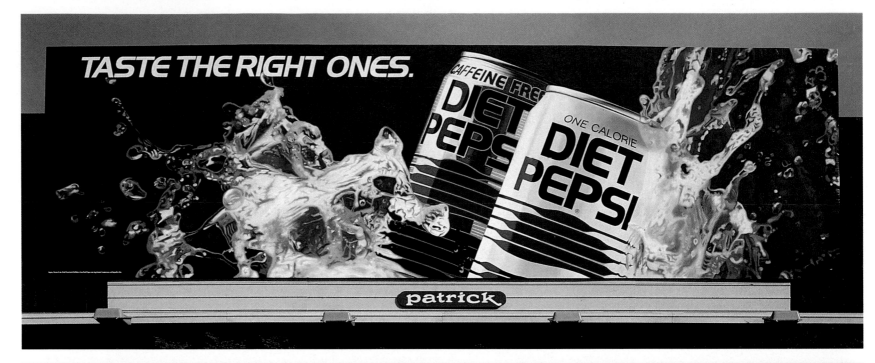

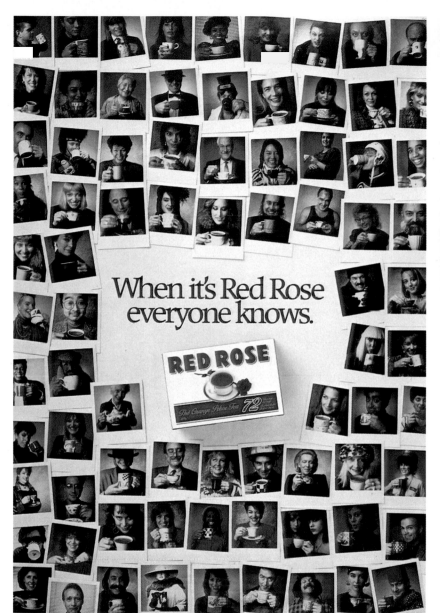

When it's Red Rose everyone knows.

RED ROSE
The Orange Pekoe Tea
72

PERRIER. WITH A TWIST.

FOSTER and KLEISER

HuggaMuggaMax

Max

Maxwell House
COFFEE
REGULAR & DECAFFEINATED

Art Directors
Derek Chapman/
Su Bundock
Designer
Derek Chapman
Design Agency
J. Walter Thompson
Toronto, Canada
Photographer
Nigel Dickson
Writer
Su Bundock
Client
T.J. Lipton
Sign
Mediacom Inc.

Art Director
James Caporimo
Design Agency
Waring & LaRosa
New York, U.S.A.
Client
Great Waters of France -
Perrier

Art Director
Jim Ronson
Designer
Jim Ronson
Design Agency
Ogilvy & Mather
Toronto, Canada
Illustrator
Roger Hill
Writer
Elly Feder
Typographer
Typsettra
Client
Kraft General Foods

Art Director
Coors Creative Services
Department
Designer
Coors Creative Services
Department
Design Agency
Coors Brewing Co.
Colorado, U.S.A.
Client
Coors Brewing Co.
Sign
Patrick Media Group

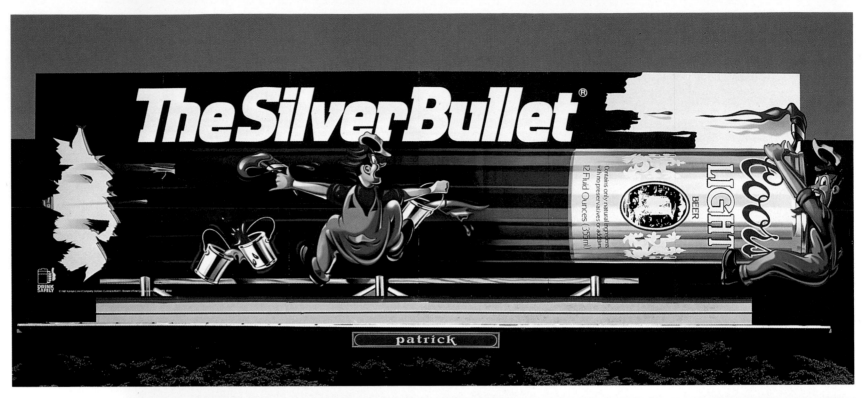

Design Agency
Backer Spielvogel &
Bates
New York, U.S.A.
Client
Miller
Sign
Patrick Media Group

Art Directors
Iain Hawk/Andy York
Designer
Iain Hawk
Design Agency
Ogilvy & Mather
Edinburgh, U.K.
Photographers
John Claridge/
Rob Wilson
Writer
Andy York
Typographer
Iain Hawk
Client
George Morton & Co.
Ltd.
Sign
Portland

The dark horse

The dark rum

The dark island

The dark rum

Scotland's No. 1

Scotland's No. 1

Creative Directors
Robert Scarpelli/
Allen Rubens
Art Director
Troy Hayes
Design Agency
DDB Needham
Worldwide
Chicago, U.S.A.
Writer
Allen Rubens
Client
Anheuser-Busch, Inc.
Sign
Eggers Films/
Patrick Media Group

Creative Director
Roy Grace
Art Director
Jillian Stern
Designer
Jillian Stern
Design Agency
Grace & Rothschild
New York, U.S.A.
Illustrator
Gerard Huerta Design
Inc.
Writer
Gary Cohen
Typographer
ROR
Client
J&B Scotch for
Paddington Corp.
Sign
Patrick Media Group

Art Directors
Terry Tomalty/
Leah Curley
Designer
Terry Tomalty
Design Agency
J. Walter Thompson
Montréal, Canada
Photographer
Peter Baumgartner
Client
Schenley Canada, Inc.
Sign
TransAd

Art Director
Derek Chapman
Designer
Derek Chapman
Design Agency
J. Walter Thompson
Toronto, Canada
Writer
Jeff Butler
Client
Fosters
Sign
Urban Outdoor

Art Director
Kurt Tauche
Designer
Pam Conboy Mariutto
Design Agency
Bozell Inc.
Minneapolis, U.S.A.
Writer
Jim Newcombe
Client
Surdyk's
Sign
Naegele Outdoor
Advertising, Inc.

Creative Director
Walt Horsfall
Art Director
Paul Brourman
Designer
Paul Brourman
Design Agency
DDB Needham
Worldwide
Chicago, U.S.A.
Photographer
Dave Jordano
Writer
Susan Gillette
Typographer
Yvette Doud
Client
Anheuser-Busch, Inc.
Sign
Spectralith, Inc./
Patrick Media Group

Art Director
Phillipe Hémono
Design Agency
Groupe Morrow
Montréal, Canada
Photographer
Michael Mills Studio
Writer
Maryse Chartrand
Typographer
Avant-Garde
Client
Brasserie Labatt -
Budweiser
Sign
P.O.S. Inc.

91

FIRE MAN'S DRINK

Art Director
Sharon Occhipinti
Designer
Sharon Occhipinti
Design Agency
DDB Needham
New York, U.S.A.
Photographer
Stuart Heir
Writer
Steve Crane
Typographer
DDB Needham
Client
Seagrams - Lord Calvert

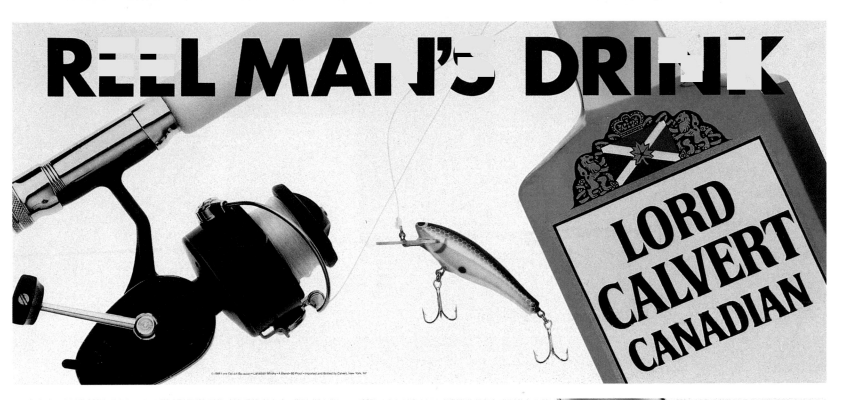

Art Director
Sharon Occhipinti
Designer
Sharon Occhipinti
Design Agency
DDB Needham
New York, U.S.A.
Photographer
Kevin Logan
Writer
Steve Crane
Typographer
DDB Needham
Client
Seagrams - Lord Calvert

Art Director
Sharon Occhipinti
Designer
Sharon Occhipinti
Design Agency
DDB Needham
New York, U.S.A.
Photographer
Nancy Ney
Writer
Steve Crane
Typographer
DDB Needham
Client
Seagrams - Lord Calvert

93

Art Director
Paul Hains
Designer
Paul Hains
Design Agency
Bozell Palmer Bonner
Toronto, Canada
Photographer
John Mastromonaco
Writer
Paul Hains
Client
Molson Breweries

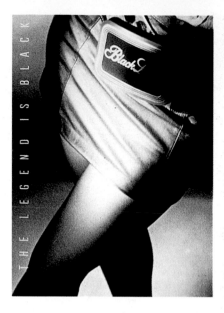

Art Director
Paul Hains
Designer
Paul Hains
Design Agency
Bozell Palmer Bonner
Toronto, Canada
Illustrator
Paul Rivoche
Writer
Paul Hains
Client
Molson Breweries

Art Director
Terry Tomalty
Designer
Terry Tomalty
Design Agency
J. Walter Thompson
Montréal, Canada
Illustrator
Roger Hill
Writer
George Walton
Client
Schenley Canada Inc.
Sign
TransAd

Creative Directors
Robert Brünig/
Karsten Frick/
Delle Krause
Design Agency
Ogilvy & Mather
Frankfurt, West Germany
Photographer
Al Satterwhite (New York)
Client
Tuborg Beer

*"He who knows the world,
knows Tuborg."*

LOCAL HEROES

HEROES' LOCAL

NORTH COUNTRY BREWERIES

Creative Director
Jeff Daniels
Designer
Jeff Daniels
Design Agency
Jeff Daniels and
Associates
Surrey, England
Photographer
Michael Joseph
Writer
Jeff Daniels
Typographer
Long John's Workshop
Client
North Country Breweries
Sign
Long John's Workshop

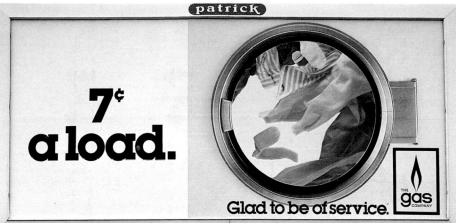

Creative Directors
Andrea Giambrone/
Veronica McLaughlin
Art Director
Veronica McLaughlin
Design Agency
John Eisaman Laws
Los Angeles, U.S.A.
Photographer
Veronica McLaughlin
Writer
Andrea Giambrone
Client
Southern California Gas
Co.
Sign
Patrick Media Group

What a 20 minute shower looks like.

Be Water Tight. ⬛ MWD METROPOLITAN WATER DISTRICT OF SOUTHERN CALIFORNIA

patrick

Creative Director
John Johnson
Art Director
Susan Fukuda
Design Agency
Gumpertz/Bentley/Fried
Los Angeles, U.S.A.
Photographer
Jeff Nadler
Writer
Felipe Bascope
Typographer
Skilset/Alpha Graphix
Client
Metropolitan Water
District of Southern
California
Sign
Patrick Media Group

CUDDLE UP WITH YOUR FLAME
Heat with lower cost GAS

GASICLE
GAS AIR CONDITIONING. 2 YEAR WARRANTY.

WARMING TREND
LOWER COST GAS HEAT.

Art Directors
Thomas Rothermel/
Bob Jaczko
Designer
Thomas Rothermel
Design Agency
Doremus & Company
Boston, U.S.A.
Illustrators
Arthur Matson/
Mike Gardiner/
Sergio Roffo

Writer
Faust Ditullio
Typographer
Display Styles/Typohouse
Client
Algonquin/Fall River Gas

Art Directors
Thomas Rothermel/
Bob Jaczko
Designer
Thomas Rothermel
Design Agency
Doremus & Company
Boston, U.S.A.
Photographer/Illustrator
Mike Gardiner/
Arthur Matson
Writer
Faust Ditullio
Typographer
Display Styles/Typohouse
Client
Algonquin/Fall River Gas
Sign
Finney Outdoor

LA FORCE DE L'ÉNERGIE
selon Élène Gamache

Gaz Métropolitain

Art Director
André Mantha
Design Agency
Groupe Morrow
Montréal, Canada
Illustrators
Elène Gamache/Riopelle/
Jean Rheault/Lisa Driver
Writer
Maryse Chartrand
Typographer
Avant-Garde
Client
Gaz Metropolitain -
Campagne "Force de
l'énergie"
Sign
Mediacom Inc.

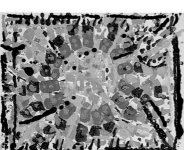

LA FORCE
DE
L'ÉNERGIE
selon Riopelle

Gaz Métropolitain

LA FORCE DE L'ÉNERGIE
selon Jean Rheault

Gaz Métropolitain

LA FORCE DE L'ÉNERGIE
selon Lisa Driver

Gaz Métropolitain

Art Director
Jeremy Carr
Designer
Jeremy Carr
Design Agency
BSB Dorland
London, England
Photographer
Mike Parsons
Writer
Jeremy Craigen
Typographer
Trevor Slabber
Client
Electricity Council

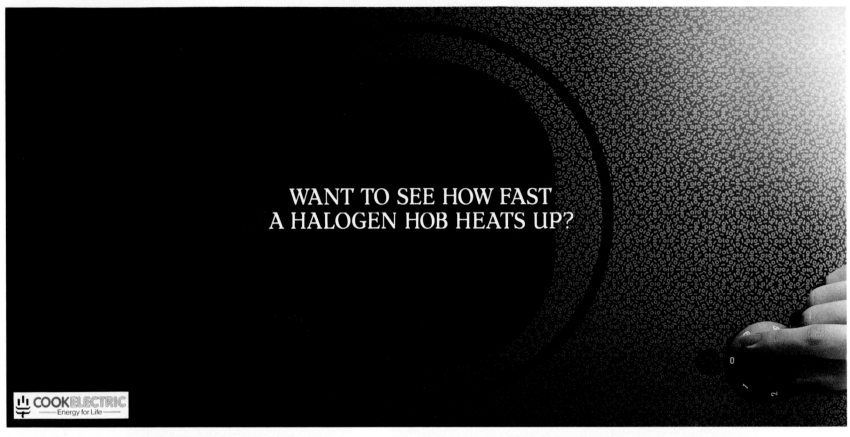

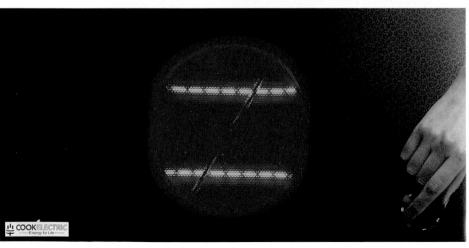

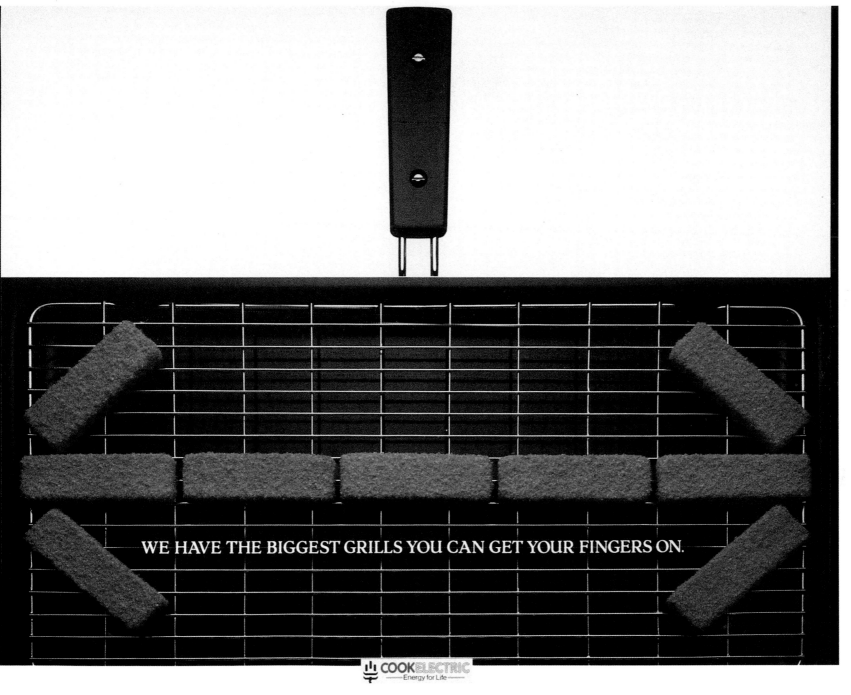

Art Director
Jeremy Carr
Designer
Jeremy Carr
Design Agency
BSB Dorland
London, England
Photographer
Mike Parsons
Writer
Jeremy Craigen
Typographer
Trevor Slabber
Client
Electricity Council

Art Director
Jeremy Carr
Designer
Jeremy Carr
Design Agency
BSB Dorland
London, England
Photographer
Hugh Johnson
Writer
Jeremy Craigen
Typographer
Trevor Slabber
Client
Electricity Council

ELECTRIC FAN OVENS WON'T LET FLAVOURS GET MIXED UP.

Art Director
Jeremy Carr
Designer
Jeremy Carr
Design Agency
BSB Dorland
London, England
Photographer
Hugh Johnson
Writer
Jeremy Craigen
Typographer
Trevor Slabber
Client
Electricity Council

105

Creative Director
Bill Borders
Art Director
Warren Eakins
Design Agency
Borders Perrin &
Norrander
Portland, U.S.A.
Photographer
Steve Bonini
Writer
Greg Eiden
Typographer
BP&N Typesetting
Client
Portland General Electric

Creative Director
Bill Borders
Art Director
Warren Eakins
Design Agency
Borders Perrin &
Norrander
Portland, U.S.A.
Photographer
Pete Stone
Writer
Dave Newman
Typographer
BP&N Typesetting
Client
Portland General Electric

Art Director
Nicole Fréchette
Designer
Robert Lebeuf
Design Agency
Publicité Martin Inc.
Montréal, Canada
Photographer/Illustrator
François Robert
Writer
Nicole Fréchette
Typographer
Avant-Garde
Client
Hydro-Québec
Sign
Mediacom Inc.

Art Directors
Steve Thursby/
Allan Kazmer
Design Agency
Carder Gray DDB
Needham
Toronto, Canada
Photographer
Terry Collier
Writer
Allan Kazmer
Typographer
Bomac
Client
Volkswagen Canada Inc.

OUTPERFORMS DEUTSCHE MARQUES.

ROVER 800 SERIES

Goeth when the iceman cometh.

SUZUKI SAMURAI

DRIVE A BMW WIDE OPEN.

patrick

MINI SPECIAL EDITION. THE QUICKEST WAY FROM 0-1960.

Art Director
Geoffrey Davidson
Designer
Geoffrey Davidson
Design Agency
Screenform Inc.
Kingston, Canada
Fabricator
Gerald Locklin & Associates
Client
General Motors of Canada/
McLaren:Lintas

Art Director
Marco Marinkovich
Designer
Marco Marinkovich
Design Agency
HKM/Rialto
Auckland, New Zealand
Writer
Marco Marinkovich
Typographer
Andrew Sims
Client
Honda New Zealand
Sign
Primesite

Art Directors
Jim Rehlin/Bill Winters
Designer
Jim Rehlin
Design Agency
Seagram & Singer
Ann Arbor, U.S.A.
Photographer
Walt Bukva
Writer
Bill Winters
Client
Toro Wheel Horse

Creative Director
Boris Damast
Art Director
Jeff Layton
Designer
Jeff Layton
Design Agency
Baker Lovick/BBDO
Toronto, Canada
Photographer
George Simhoni
Writer
Boris Damast
Typographer
The Composing Room
Client
Chrysler Canada Ltd.
Sign
Mediacom Inc.

Art Director
Andy Ward
Designer
Andy Ward
Design Agency
BSB Dorland
London, England
Photographer
Martin Thompson
Writer
James Von Leyden
Typographer
Trevor Slabber
Client
Rover Cars

Art Director
Jeff Layton
Designer
Jeff Layton
Design Agency
Jeff Layton & Assoc. Ltd./
Grey Canada
Toronto, Canada
Photographer
Bill McLeod
Writers
Jeff Layton/Gerry Cooper
Typographer
Typsettra Ltd.
Client
Quaker State
Sign
H&S Reliance/Trans Ad

Creative Director
Boris Damast
Art Director
Jeff Layton
Designer
Jeff Layton
Design Agency
Baker Lovick/BBDO
Toronto, Canada
Photographer
George Simhoni
Writer
Boris Damast
Typographer
The Composing Room
Client
Chrysler Canada Ltd.
Sign
Mediacom Inc.

Love.

Love letter.

Car caring people reach for the best.

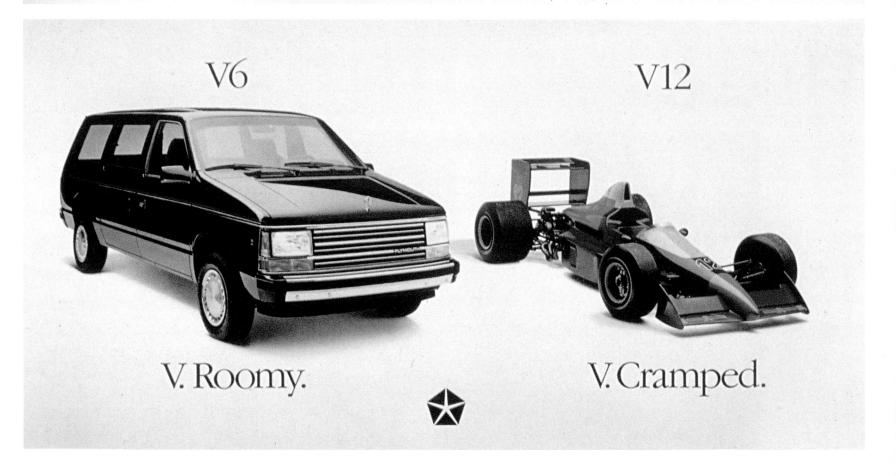

112

The fear of other liftbacks is coming.

THE NEW HONDA CONCERTO. FROM $27,990

226

A TOUCH, TOUCH, TOUCH OF CLASS.

25 TXE

THE NEW RENAULT 25 TXE 2·0 INJECTION.

THERE'S MORE TO LIFE WITH RENAULT

WHY SHOULD YOUR BOSS GET ALL THE PERKS? THE ROVER 820e, £13,185.

Art Director
Marco Marinkovich
Designer
Marco Marinkovich
Design Agency
HKM/Rialto
Auckland, New Zealand
Photographer
Dave Whorwood
Writer
Marco Marinkovich
Typographer
Mark Hunter
Client
Honda New Zealand
Sign
Primesite

Creative Director
Tim Mellors
Art Director
Digby Atkinson
Design Agency
Publicis
London, England
Photographer
Martin Thompson
Writer
Chris Waite
Typographer
Ros Walter
Client
Renault UK Limited

Art Director
Colin Bebrouth
Designer
Colin Bebrouth
Design Agency
BSB Dorland
London, England
Photographer
Ken Griffiths
Writer
Alan Lofthouse
Typographer
Trevor Slabber
Client
Rover Cars

Art Directors
Brian Harrod/James Jung
Design Agency
Harrod & Mirlin
Toronto, Canada
Photographer
Barry Johnson
Writers
Ian Mirlin/
Brian Harrod/Clive
Desmond
Client
Ian Flynn–Suzuki Canada
Sign
Hook Outdoor
Advertising

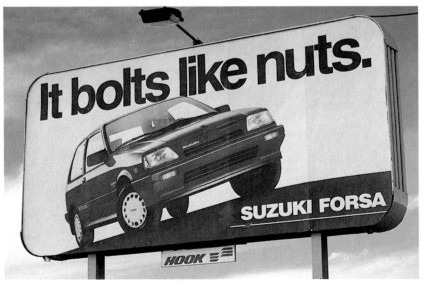

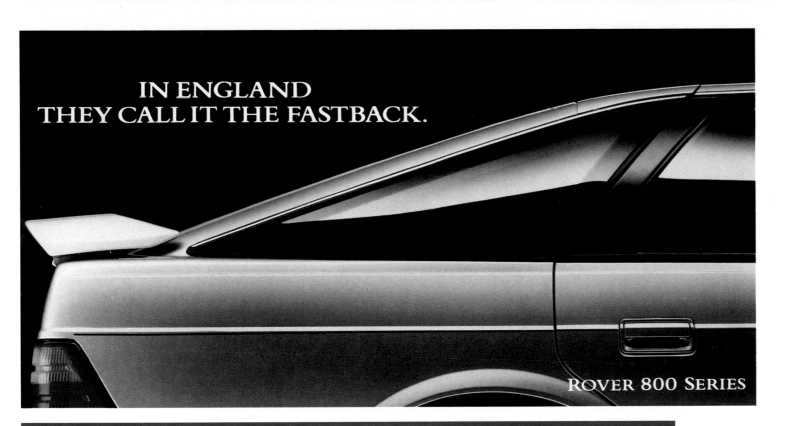

IN ENGLAND
THEY CALL IT THE FASTBACK.

ROVER 800 SERIES

Coupe du Jour.

Accord LXi Coupe
HONDA

patrick

Art Director
Dave Palmer
Designer
Dave Palmer
Design Agency
BSB Dorland
London, England
Photographer
Paul Bevitt
Writer
Barry Whitehead
Typographer
Trevor Slabber
Client
Rover Cars

Creative Director
Larry Postaer
Designer
Gary Yoshida
Design Agency
Rubin, Postaer &
Associates
Los Angeles, U.S.A.
Photographer
Jim Hall
Writer
Bob Coburn
Typographer
Lovellen Nanda
Client
Honda
Sign
Patrick Media Group

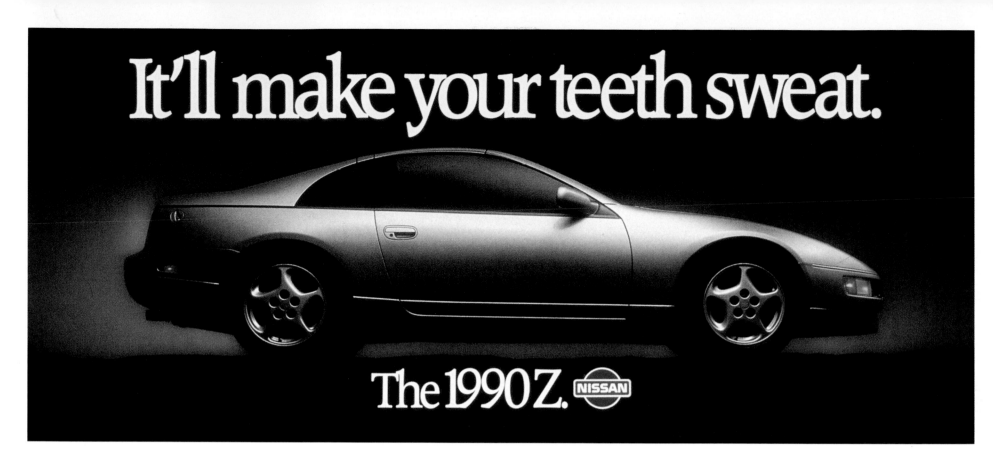

Creative & Art Director
Geoffrey B. Roche
Design Agency
Chiat/Day/Mojo inc.
Advertising
Toronto, Canada
Photographer
Robert Grigg
Writer
Terry O'Reilly
Client
Nissan

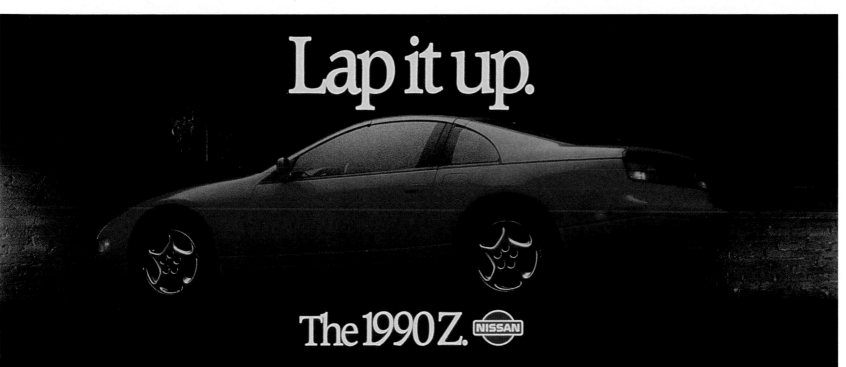

Creative & Art Director
Geoffrey B. Roche
Design Agency
Chiat/Day/Mojo inc.
Advertising
Toronto, Canada
Writer
Terry O'Reilly
Client
Nissan

Creative Director
Ken Weiden
Art Director
Randy Diplock
Design Agency
Chiat/Day/Mojo inc.
Advertising
Toronto, Canada
Photographer
The Designery
Writer
Terry O'Reilly
Typographer
Canadian Composition
Client
Nissan

Creative Director
Neil McGregor
Art Director
Lizanne L'Africain
Designer
Lizanne L'Africain
Design Agency
MacLaren:Lintas
Advertising
Montréal, Canada
Photographer
Marc Drolet
Writer
Jacques Davidts
Typographer
Charles LeBlanc
Client
ADHOC (Service
Placement)
Sign
P.O.S. Inc.

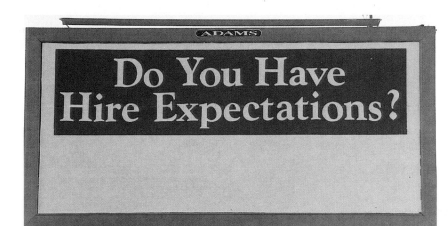

Art Director
Sandy Shuler
Design Agency
Adams Outdoor
Advertising
Norfolk, U.S.A.
Writers
Sandy Shuler/
Marci Waltower
Client
Sun Personnel
Sign
Ken Hill

Art Director
Marci Waltower
Design Agency
Adams Outdoor
Advertising
Norfolk, U.S.A.
Writers
Marci Waltower/
Sandy Shuler
Client
Reliance Temporary
Service
Sign
Vincent Printing Co.

Art Director
Kurt Tauche
Designer
Jeff Terwilliger
Design Agency
Bozell Inc.
Minneapolis, U.S.A.
Writer
Dick Thomas
Client
Star Tribune

120

Art Director
Bert Gardner
Designer
Craig Tanimoto
Design Agency
Bozell Inc.
Minneapolis, U.S.A.
Writer
John Francis
Client
Star Tribune

Art Director
Bert Gardner
Designer
Mike Gustafson
Design Agency
Bozell Inc.
Minneapolis, U.S.A.
Illustrator
Chris Grajczyk
Writer
Bruce Hannum
Client
Star Tribune

Art Director
Bert Gardner
Designer
Mike Gustafson
Design Agency
Bozell Inc.
Minneapolis, U.S.A.
Illustrator
Chris Grajczyk
Writer
Dick Thomas
Client
Star Tribune

Art Director
Kurt Tauche
Designer
Gregg Byers
Design Agency
Bozell Inc.
Minneapolis, U.S.A.
Fabricator
Prop Shop
Writer
Bruce Hannum
Client
Star Tribune

Art Director
Kurt Tauche
Designer
Gregg Byers
Design Agency
Bozell Inc.
Minneapolis, U.S.A.
Writer
John Francis
Client
Star Tribune

Art Director
Kurt Tauche
Designer
Pam Conboy Mariutto
Design Agency
Bozell Inc.
Minneapolis, U.S.A.
Illustrator
Mike Reed
Writer
Kerry Casey
Client
Star Tribune

Art Director
Kurt Tauche
Designer
Jeff Jones
Design Agency
Bozell Inc.
Minneapolis, U.S.A.
Writer
Bruce Hannum
Client
Star Tribune

123

It puts any seat on the 50 yard line.

Expert Advice On Playing The Field.

Every Edition's An Extra.

Hard Hitting Football Coverage.

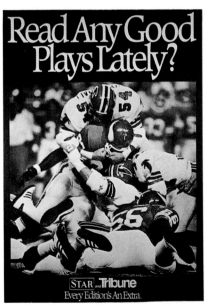

Read Any Good Plays Lately?

Every Edition's An Extra.

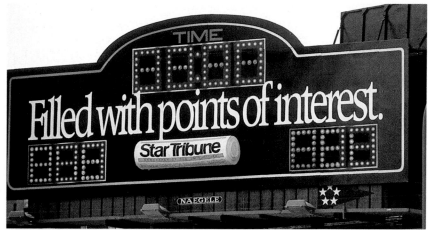

Art Director
Kurt Tauche
Designer
Gregg Byers
Design Agency
Bozell Inc.
Minneapolis, U.S.A.
Writer
Dick Thomas
Client
Star Tribune

Art Director
Kurt Tauche
Designer
Pam Conboy Mariutto
Design Agency
Bozell Inc.
Minneapolis, U.S.A.
Writer
Kerry Casey
Client
Star Tribune

Art Director
Kurt Tauche
Designer
Pam Conboy Mariutto
Design Agency
Bozell Inc.
Minneapolis, U.S.A.
Writer
Kerry Casey
Client
Star Tribune

Art Director
Bert Gardner
Designer
Jeff Terwilliger
Design Agency
Bozell Inc.
Minneapolis, U.S.A.
Writer
Pete Pohl
Client
Star Tribune

Art Director
Kurt Tauche
Designer
Jeff Terwilliger
Design Agency
Bozell Inc.
Minneapolis, U.S.A.
Writer
Glen Wachowiak
Client
Star Tribune

We never miss an issue
Neither should you

EVERY ISSUE FULL OF ISSUES ■ EVERY THURSDAY

We never miss an issue
Neither should you

EVERY ISSUE FULL OF ISSUES ■ EVERY THURSDAY

We never miss an issue
Neither should you

EVERY ISSUE FULL OF ISSUES ■ EVERY THURSDAY

We never miss an issue
Neither should you

EVERY ISSUE FULL OF ISSUES ■ EVERY THURSDAY

Creative Director
Jac Coverdale
Art Director
David Fox
Design Agency
Clarity Coverdale Rueff
Advertising, Inc.
Minneapolis, U.S.A.
Photographer
Paul Sinkler
Writer
Joe Alexander
Typographer
Great Faces
Client
St. Paul Pioneer Press
Sign
Naegele Outdoor
Advertising, Inc.

Creative Director
Jac Coverdale
Designer
Jac Coverdale
Design Agency
Clarity Coverdale Rueff
Advertising, Inc.
Minneapolis, U.S.A.
Photographer
Paul Sinkler
Writer
Joe Alexander
Typographer
Great Faces
Client
St. Paul Pioneer Press
Sign
Naegele Outdoor
Advertising, Inc.

Creative Director
Jac Coverdale
Designer
Jac Coverdale
Design Agency
Clarity Coverdale Rueff
Advertising, Inc.
Minneapolis, U.S.A.
Illustrator
Bob Peters
Writer
Joe Alexander
Typographer
Great Faces
Client
St. Paul Pioneer Press
Sign
Naegele Outdoor
Advertising, Inc.

Creative Director
Jac Coverdale
Designer
Jac Coverdale
Design Agency
Clarity Coverdale Rueff
Advertising, Inc.
Minneapolis, U.S.A.
Illustrator
Bill Bruning
Writer
Joe Alexander
Typographer
Great Faces
Client
St. Paul Pioneer Press
Sign
Naegele Outdoor
Advertising, Inc.

Creative Director
Jac Coverdale
Designer
Jac Coverdale
Design Agency
Clarity Coverdale Rueff
Advertising, Inc.
Minneapolis, U.S.A.
Illustrator
Leland Klanderman
Writer
Joe Alexander
Typographer
Great Faces
Client
St. Paul Pioneer Press
Sign
Naegele Outdoor
Advertising, Inc.

Creative Director
Jac Coverdale
Designer
Jac Coverdale
Design Agency
Clarity Coverdale Rueff
Advertising, Inc.
Photographer
Paul Sinkler
Writer
Jerry Fury
Typographer
Great Faces
Client
St. Paul Pioneer Press
Sign
Naegele Outdoor
Advertising, Inc.

Art Director
Jeff Jackson
Designers
Jeff Jackson/David Ham
Design Agency
Reed Ham Jackson, Inc.
San Antonio, U.S.A.
Writer
David Ham
Client
The San Antonio
Express-News/Murdoch
Corp.
Sign
The Robert Keith
Company

Art Directors
Richard Cristo/
Dennis Lim/
David Toyoshima
Design Agency
Ketchum
Communications
Los Angeles, U.S.A.
Photographer
Michael Jacobs
Writer
Martin MacDonald
Typographer
Andresen
Client
Herald Examiner
Sign
Patrick Media Group

Art Director
Steve Penchina
Designer
Richie Goldstein
Design Agency
Impact Outdoor
Advertising Co.
Dallas, U.S.A.
Photographer
Wally McNamee
Writer
Steve Penchina
Client
Newsweek–Bill Bergman
Sign
Impact Outdoor/Patrick
Media Group

Art Director/Designer
Gaynor Notman
Design Agency
BSB Dorland
London, England
Photographer
John Swannel
Writer
Peter Smith
Typographer
Trevor Slabber
Client
Express Newspapers

Creative Director
Andrew Cracknell
Designer
Stuart Wilson
Design Agency
BSB Dorland
London, England
Illustrator
Stock Shot
Writer
Noel Sharmon
Typographer
Martin Tillbrook
Client
Sunday Express
Newspaper

Art Director
Dave Palmer
Designer
Dave Palmer
Design Agency
BSB Dorland
London, England
Photographer
John Thornton
Writer
Barry Whitehead
Typographer
Trevor Slabber
Client
Sunday Express
Newspaper

Art Director
Dave Palmer
Designer
Dave Palmer
Design Agency
BSB Dorland
London, England
Photographer
Don McCullen
Writer
Barry Whitehead
Typographer
Trevor Slabber
Client
Sunday Express
Newspaper

132

We're there for you, every day

Los Angeles Times

Art Director
John Keuning
Design Agency
J. Walter Thompson
Los Angeles, U.S.A.
Copywriter
Ernie Kloetzli
Client
Los Angeles Times
Sign
Patrick Media Group

Art Director
Sam Hurford
Design Agency
Publicis
London, England
Photographer
Rex Features
Writer
Julian Dyer
Typographer
Leon Butcher
Client
The Guardian

*The***Prince** and *The***Architect.**

February 3

A royal view of the modern world. *The***Weekend.**

133

Art Director
Gus Pitsikoulis
Designer
Gus Pitsikoulis
Design Agency
Babbit & Reiman
Advertising
Atlanta, U.S.A.
Illustrators
McLean & Friends/
Martin Pate
Writer
Ralph McGill
Typographer
Characters
Client
Atlanta Jewish Times
Sign
Adams Outdoor

Art Director
Steve Jones
Design Agency
McCann-Erickson
Manchester, England
Writer
Steve Mees
Client
Next Directory

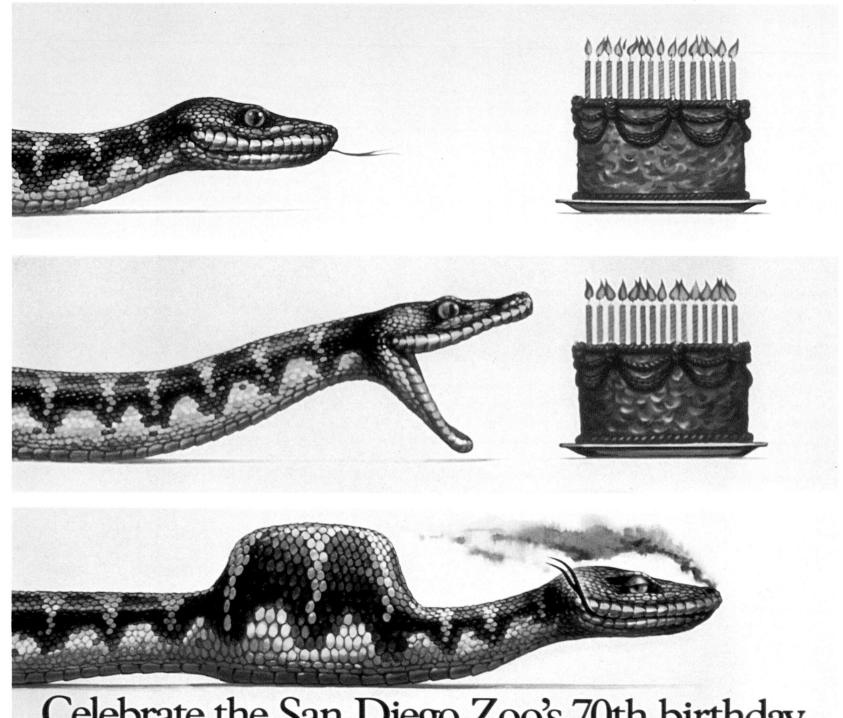

Art Director
Bob Kwait
Designer
Bob Kwait
Design Agency
Phillips-Ramsey
San Diego, U.S.A.
Illustrator
Darrel Millsap
Writer
Bob Kwait
Typographer
CRT Type
Client
San Diego Zoo
Sign
Gannett

Celebrate the San Diego Zoo's 70th birthday.

Celebrate the San Diego Zoo's 70th birthday.

Art Director
Bob Kwait
Designer
Bob Kwait
Design Agency
Phillips-Ramsey
San Diego, U.S.A.
Illustrator
Darrel Millsap
Writer
Rich Badami
Typographer
Laurie Dotson
Client
San Diego Zoo
Sign
Gangi Studios Inc./
Benline

Art Director
Bob Kwait
Designer
Bob Kwait
Design Agency
Phillips-Ramsey
San Diego, U.S.A.
Illustrator
Darrel Millsap
Writer
Bob Kwait
Typographer
Laurie Dotson
Client
San Diego Zoo
Sign
Gangi Studios Inc./
Benline

The San Diego Zoo

70 years and still kicking.

The latest rage.

Tiger River. The San Diego Zoo

Art Director
Bob Kwait
Designer
Bob Kwait
Design Agency
Phillips-Ramsey
San Diego, U.S.A.
Illustrator
Darrel Millsap
Writer
Lynn Macey
Typographer
Laurie Dotson
Client
San Diego Zoo
Sign
Gangi Studios Inc./
Benline

Tiger River.

A new twist.

At the San Diego

Art Director
Bob Kwait
Designer
Bob Kwait
Design Agency
Phillips-Ramsey
San Diego, U.S.A.
Illustrator
Darrel Millsap
Writer
Lynn Macey
Typographer
CRT Type
Client
San Diego Zoo
Sign
Gannett

The world's greatest zoo is in your neck of the woods.

San Diego Zoo

Art Director
Bob Kwait
Designer
Bob Kwait
Design Agency
Phillips-Ramsey
San Diego, U.S.A.
Illustrator
Darrel Millsap
Writer
Bob Kwait
Typographer
CRT Type
Client
San Diego Zoo
Sign
Gangi Studios

140

See you later.

The San Diego Zoo

Art Director
Bob Kwait
Designer
Bob Kwait
Design Agency
Phillips-Ramsey
San Diego, U.S.A.
Illustrator
Darrel Millsap
Writer
Bob Kwait
Typographer
CRT Type
Client
San Diego Zoo
Sign
Gangi Studios

Double-deck bus tours.

The San Diego Zoo

Make my day.

Visit the San Diego Zoo.

Art Director
Bob Kwait
Designer
Bob Kwait
Design Agency
Phillips-Ramsey
San Deigo, U.S.A.
Writer
Rich Badami
Typographer
Laurie Dotson
Client
San Diego Zoo
Sign
Gangi Studios/Benline

Art Director
Bob Kwait
Designer
Bob Kwait
Design Agency
Phillips-Ramsey
San Diego, U.S.A.
Illustrator
Darrel Millsap
Photographer
Ron Garrison
Writers
Bob Kwait/Rich Badami
Typographer
CRT Type
Client
San Diego Zoo
Sign
Gannett/Gangi Studios

The hip place to go.

The San Diego Zoo

A rare tweet.

The
San Diego
Zoo

Never a dull moment.

The
San Diego
Zoo

Art Director
Bob Kwait
Designer
Bob Kwait
Design Agency
Phillips-Ramsey
San Diego, U.S.A.
Illustrator
Darrel Millsap
Writers
Bob Kwait/Rich Badami
Typographer
CRT Type
Client
San Diego Zoo
Sign
Gangi Studios

70 years and in the pink.

The
San Diego
Zoo

Art Director
Bob Kwait
Designer
Bob Kwait
Design Agency
Phillips-Ramsey
San Diego, U.S.A.
Illustrator
Darrel Millsap
Writer
Bob Kwait
Typographer
CRT Type
Client
San Diego Zoo
Sign
Gannett

Unforgettable.
The San Diego Zoo.

The world's greatest zoo is right in your own back yard.

San Diego Zoo

Art Director
Bob Kwait
Designer
Bob Kwait
Design Agency
Phillips-Ramsey
San Diego, U.S.A.
Illustrator
Darrel Millsap
Writer
Bob Kwait
Typographer
Laurie Dotson
Client
San Diego Zoo
Sign
Gangi Studios/Benline

Art Director
Bob Kwait
Designer
Bob Kwait
Design Agency
Phillips-Ramsey
San Diego, U.S.A.
Illustrator
Darrel Millsap
Writers
Bob Kwait/Dave Bradley
Typographer
CRT Type
Client
San Diego Zoo
Sign
Gangi Studios

The talk of the town.

Tiger River
The San Diego Zoo

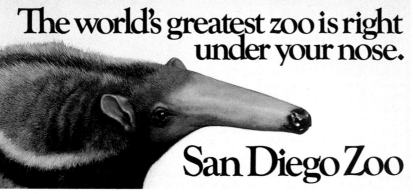

The world's greatest zoo is right under your nose.

San Diego Zoo

You won't believe your eyes.

Tiger River.
New at the San Diego Zoo

The family that preys together.

The
San Diego
Zoo

Look before they leave.

The
San Diego
Zoo

Art Director
Bob Kwait
Designer
Bob Kwait
Design Agency
Phillips-Ramsey
San Diego, U.S.A.
Illustrator
Darrel Millsap
Writer
Bob Kwait
Typographer
Laurie Dotson
Client
San Diego Zoo
Sign
Gangi Studios/Benline

Art Director
Bob Kwait
Designer
Bob Kwait
Design Agency
Phillips-Ramsey
San Diego, U.S.Λ.
Illustrator
Darrel Millsap
Writer
Bob Kwait
Typographer
Laurie Dotson
Client
San Diego Zoo
Sign
Gangi Studios/Benline

Art Director
Bob Kwait
Designer
Bob Kwait
Design Agency
Phillips-Ramsey
San Diego, U.S.A.
Illustrator
Darrel Millsap
Writer
Bob Kwait
Typographer
CRT Type
Client
San Diego Zoo
Sign
Gangi Studios

The Cincinnati Zoo Just Struck Gold.

Golden Monkeys From China.

Art Director
Dave Bukvic
Designer
Donna Routt
Design Agency
Mann Bukvic Associates
Cincinnati, U.S.A.
Illustrator
David Groff
Writer
Dave Bukvic
Client
Cincinnati Zoo
Sign
Norton Outdoor
Advertising

Art Director
Teresa Newberry
Designer
Teresa Newberry
Design Agency
Mann Bukvic Associates
Cincinnati, U.S.A.
Illustrator
Tom Szumowski
Writer
Karla Weller
Typographer
Q.C. Type Inc.
Client
Cincinnati Zoo
Sign
Norton Outdoor
Advertising

Art Director
Teresa Newberry
Designer
Teresa Newberry
Design Agency
Mann Bukvic Associates
Cincinnati, U.S.A.
Illustrator
Doug Henry
Writer
Debbie Effler
Typographer
Q.C. Type Inc.
Client
Cincinnati Zoo
Sign
Norton Outdoor
Advertising

Art Director
Teresa Newberry
Designer
Teresa Newberry
Design Agency
Mann Bukvic Associates
Cincinnati, U.S.A.
Illustrator
Ken Goldammer
Writer
Dave Bukvic
Client
Cincinnati Zoo
Sign
Norton Outdoor
Advertising

Art Director
Dave Bukvic
Designer
Donna Routt
Design Agency
Mann Bukvic Associates
Cincinnati, U.S.A.
Illustrator
David Groff
Writer
Dave Bukvic
Client
Cincinnati Zoo
Sign
Norton Outdoor
Advertising

CHEEP. THE GREAT L.A. ZOO $2⁰⁰ KIDS $4⁵⁰ ADULTS

patrick

WAVE IF YOU LIKE THE SEATTLE AQUARIUM

A Public Service Donation by Ackerley Communications of the Northwest

ACKERLEY

ACKERLEY

See the Snow Leopard.
While supplies last.

Endangered Species Month. Woodland Park Zoo.

A PUBLIC SERVICE DONATION BY ACKERLEY COMMUNICATIONS OF THE NORTHWEST

Art Director
Mikio Osaki
Designer
Mikio Osaki
Design Agency
Poindexter/Osaki/
Nissman
Los Angeles, U.S.A.
Illustrator
Brian Zick
Writer
Mikio Osaki
Typographer
Andresen
Client
The Los Angeles Zoo
Sign
Patrick Media Group

Art Director
Ron Hansen
Designer
Ron Hansen
Design Agency
Ackerley
Communications of the
Northwest, Inc.
Seattle, U.S.A.
Illustrator
Bart Bemus
Writers
Ron Hansen/Ed
Leinbacher
Typographer
Thomas and Kennedy
Client
Seattle Aquarium
Sign
Ackerley
Communications of the
Northwest, Inc.

Art Directors
Matt Myers/Jim Copacino
Designers
Matt Myers/Jim Copacino
Design Agency
Ackerley
Communications of the
Northwest, Inc.
Seattle, U.S.A.
Illustrator
Scott Vincent
Typographer
Thomas and Kennedy
Client
Woodland Park Zoo
Sign
Ackerley
Communications of the
Northwest, Inc.

Creative Director
Geoffrey B. Roche
Art Directors
Geoffrey B. Roche/
Duncan Milner
Design Agency
Chiat/Day/Mojo inc.
Advertising
Toronto, Canada
Illustrator
Doug Martin
Writer
Joe Alexander
Typographer
Word for Word/
Stuart Freedman
Client
Metro Toronto Zoo

152

Creative & Art Director
Geoffrey B. Roche
Design Agency
Chiat/Day/Mojo inc.
Advertising
Toronto, Canada
Illustrator
Doug Martin
Writer
Joe Alexander
Typographer
Word for Word/
Stuart Freedman
Client
Metro Toronto Zoo

Creative Director
Paul Waddell
Designers
Susan Westre/
Dorothy Allard
Design Agency
Evans
Los Angeles, U.S.A.
Writer
Bill Schohl
Client
Marineland
Sign
Patrick Media Group

154

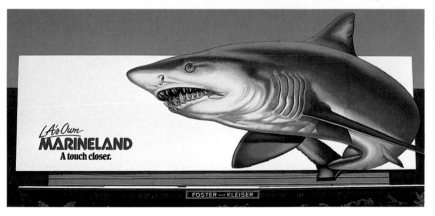

Creative Director
Paul Waddell
Designers
Susan Westre/
Dorothy Allard
Design Agency
Evans
Los Angeles, U.S.A.
Writer
Bill Schohl
Client
Marineland

Creative Director
John Armistead
Art Director
Jeff Weekley
Design Agency
DMB&B
Los Angeles, U.S.A.
Illustrator
Gary Norman
Writer
Gary Alpern
Typographer
Aldus Type Studio
Client
Sea World of California
Sign
Patrick Media Group

Art Director
Paul Waddell
Designers
Susan Westre/
Dorothy Allard
Design Agency
Evans
Los Angeles, U.S.A.
Writer
Bill Schohl
Client
Marineland

STRAIGHT AHEAD TO LOUISIANA DOWNS.

Art Director
Bob Kwait
Designer
Bob Kwait
Design Agency
Phillips-Ramsey
San Diego, U.S.A.
Photographer
Michael Balderas
Writer
Bob Kwait
Typographer
Laurie Dotson
Client
Louisiana Downs
Sign
Metromedia
Technologies

Art Director
Bob Kwait
Designer
Bob Kwait
Design Agency
Phillips-Ramsey,
San Diego, U.S.A.
Photographer
Art Fox
Writer
Rich Badami
Typographer
Laurie Dotson
Client
Louisiana Downs
Sign
Gangi Studios/Benline

Make Money The Old-Fashioned Way. Win It.

Louisiana Downs

TURN AROUND. YOU'VE MISSED LOUISIANA DOWNS.

GOOD NEWS TRAVELS FAST.

Del Mar Opens July 23

Art Director
Bob Kwait
Designer
Bob Kwait
Design Agency
Phillips Ramsey
San Diego, U.S.A.
Photographer
Michael Balderas
Writer
Bob Kwait
Typographer
Laurie Dotson
Client
Louisiana Downs
Sign
Metromedia
Technologies

Art Director
John Vitro
Designer
John Vitro
Design Agency
Phillips-Ramsey
San Diego, U.S.A.
Writer
John Robertson
Typographer
Laurie Dotson
Client
Del Mar Thoroughbred
Club
Sign
Gangi Studios/Benline

Art Director
Bob Kwait
Designer
Bob Kwait
Design Agency
Phillips-Ramsey
San Diego, U.S.A.
Illustrator
Darrel Millsap
Writer
Tony Durket
Typographer
CRT Type
Client
Louisiana Downs
Sign
Gannett

THE HOOFBEAT
OF AMERICA.

LOUISIANA DOWNS

Six Appeal

Bet the Super Six at Louisiana Downs

1p.m.post/Fri.3p.m.

The Joy of Six

Bet the Super Six at Louisiana Downs

Opens April 26

Six Therapy

Bet the Super Six at Louisiana Downs

1p.m.post/Fri.3p.m.

The horses return to Del Mar July 26.

Art Director
Bob Kwait
Designer
Bob Kwait
Design Agency
Phillips-Ramsey
San Diego, U.S.A.
Illustrator
Darrel Millsap
Writers
Rich Badami/Bob Kwait
Typographer
CRT Type
Client
Louisiana Downs
Sign
Gangi Studios

Art Directors
Duncan Milner/Bob Kwait
Designer
Duncan Milner
Design Agency
Phillips-Ramsey
San Diego, U.S.A.
Illustrator
Marshall Harrington
Writer
Cam Davis
Typographer
CRT Type
Client
Del Mar Thoroughbred
Club
Sign
Gangi Studios

HUNCHES SERVED DAILY.

LOUISIANA DOWNS. RACING WEDNESDAY THRU SUNDAY.

Art Director
Bob Kwait
Designer
Bob Kwait
Design Agency
Phillips-Ramsey
San Diego, U.S.A.
Photographer
Marshall Harrington
Writer
Bob Kwait
Typographer
Laurie Dotson
Client
Louisiana Downs
Sign
Gangi Studios/Benline

GO TO YELL.

LOUISIANA DOWNS

Art Director
Bob Kwait
Designer
Bob Kwait
Design Agency
Phillips-Ramsey
San Diego, U.S.A.
Photographer
Marshall Harrington
Writer
Lynn Macey
Typographer
Laurie Dotson
Client
Louisiana Downs
Sign
Gangi Studios/Benline

Art Director
John Vitro
Designer
John Vitro
Design Agency
Phillips-Ramsey
San Diego, U.S.A.
Writer
John Robertson
Typographer
Laurie Dotson
Client
Del Mar Thoroughbred
Club
Sign
Gangi Studios/Benline

AFTER SEPT. 10 THEY MAKE A FAST GETAWAY.

Del Mar

Art Director
Doug Lew
Design Agency
Chuck Ruhr Advertising
Minneapolis, U.S.A.
Writer
Bill Johnson
Client
Canterbury Downs

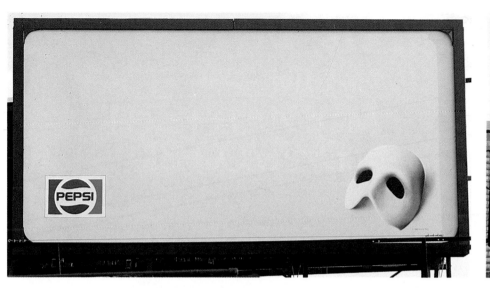

Art Directors
Gray Abraham/
Colin Priestley
Designers
Gray Abraham/
Colin Priestley
Design Agency
J. Walter Thompson
Toronto, Canada
Illustrator
Ken Walley
Writer
Brent Pulford
Client
Pepsico Canada
Sign
Mediacom Inc.

163

Art Director
Doug Lew
Design Agency
Chuck Ruhr Advertising
Minneapolis, U.S.A.
Writer
Bob Thacker
Client
Minneapolis Institute of
Arts

Art Director
Doug Lew
Design Agency
Chuck Ruhr Advertising
Minneapolis, U.S.A.
Writer
Bill Johnson
Client
Minneapolis Institute of
Arts

Famous faces turn up every day.

)(LAS VEGAS HILTON POKER ROOM

)(LAS VEGAS HILTON   NOW OPEN

SUPERBOOK

Art Director
Kevin McCarthy
Designer
Kevin McCarthy
Design Agency
Phillips-Ramsey
San Diego, U.S.A.
Photographer
Marshall Harrington
Writer
Brian Belefant
Client
Las Vegas Hilton

Art Director
Bob Kwait
Designer
Bob Kwait
Design Agency
Phillips-Ramsey
San Diego, U.S.A.
Photographer
Art Fox
Writer
Bob Kwait
Typographer
CRT Type
Client
Las Vegas Hilton
Sign
Gannett

This 220 lb. Norwegian has a chilling thought for Michael Spinks.

SPINKS VS. TANGSTAD

SEPT. 6)(LAS VEGAS HILTON

VINDICATION
IN VEGAS.
SPINKS VS. HOLMES
LAS VEGAS HILTON
APR. 19

Art Director
Rob Richards
Designer
Rob Richards
Design Agency
Gannett Outdoor of
Arizona
Phoenix, U.S.A.
Client
KNXV-TV 15/Phoenix
Sign
Gannett Outdoor of
Arizona

Art Directors
Leif Nielsen/Allan Kazmer
Design Agency
Carder Gray DDB
Needham
Toronto, Canada
Photographer
Ian Campbell
Writer
Steve Conover
Typographer
H & S Reliance Ltd.
Client
Chieftain Products Inc.

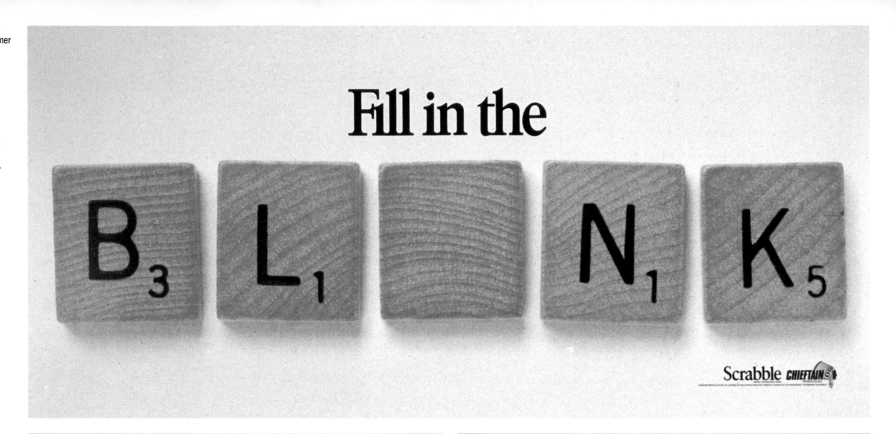

168

Art Director
Nancy Rowland
Designers
Nancy Rowland/
Robert Lyles
Design Agency
AM710 KMPC
Los Angeles, U.S.A.
Writer
Robert Lyles
Typographer
Nancy Rowland
Client
AM710 KMPC
Sign
Patrick Media Group

Creative Director
Peter Coutroulis
Art Director
David Heise
Design Agency
Davis Ball & Colombatto
Los Angeles, U.S.A.
Illustrator
Schultz
Writer
Tammy Tinkler
Typographer
Andresen
Client
Knott's Berry Farm

Art Director
Ian Banner
Design Agency
Barrington Johnson
Lorains
Manchester, England
Illustrator
John Richardson
Writer
David Harrison
Typographer
Amanda Banner
Client
Granada Studios Tour

Art Director
Pam Conboy Mariutto
Design Agency
Martin/Williams
Advertising
Minneapolis, U.S.A.
Writer
Lyle Wedemeyer
Client
Skipper's Seafood -
Chowder House

Art Director
John Sayles
Designer
John Sayles
Design Agency
Sayles Graphic Design,
Inc.
Des Moines, U.S.A.
Writer
Mary Langen-Goldstien
Client
The Pier
Sign
Naegele Outdoor
Advertising, Inc.

Art Director
Kim Kirkhart
Designer
Kim Kirkhart
Design Agency
Michael & Partners
Dallas, U.S.A.
Illustrator
George Toomer
Writer
Michal Lawrence
Typographer
SW Typographics
Client
The Black-eyed Pea
Sign
3M

Art Director
Marco Marinkovich
Designer
James Mok
Design Agency
HKM/Rialto
Auckland, New Zealand
Photographer
James Mok
Writer
Peter Fantl
Typographer
James Mok
Client
Azcorp Corporation
Sign
Primesite

Creative Director
Jack Higgins
Art Director
Tamara Johnson
Designer
Tamara Johnson
Design Agency
Ehrig and Associates
Seattle, U.S.A.
Photographer
Darrell Peterson
Writer
Vince Beggin
Typographer
Thomas & Kennedy
Client
Lake Ballinger Athletic
Club
Sign
Ackerley
Communications

Art Director
Jeff Jackson
Designer
Jeff Jackson
Design Agency
Reed Ham Jackson, Inc.
San Antonio, U.S.A.
Photographer
Constance Ashley
Writer
Jeff Jackson/David Ham
Typographer
Dennis Fetterman/
Pro-Type
Client
Gary Pools, Inc.
Sign
Patrick Media Group

Art Director
Robert Moore
Designer
Robert Moore
Design Agency
W.S.I., Camarillo, U.S.A.
Photographer
WM Hendricks Studio
Writer
Steven Miller
Typographer
Super Type
Client
I. Martin Imports
Sign
Gannett Outdoor

Art Directors
Keith Ogorek/
Jennifer Meyers
Designer
Jennifer Meyers
Design Agency
Williams Company
Terre Haute, U.S.A.
Photographer
Tim Summerville
Writer
Keith Ogorek
Typographer
Terre Haute Engraving
Client
Forrest Sherer Insurance
Sign
Whiteco

Creative Director
Keith Ogorek
Designer
Neil Garrison
Design Agency
Williams Company
Terre Haute, U.S.A.
Writer
Keith Ogorek
Typographer
Phil's Photo
Client
Methodist Sports
Medicine Center

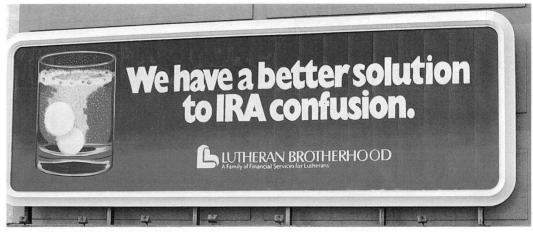

Art Director
Bert Gardner
Designer
Craig Tanimoto
Design Agency
Bozell Inc.
Minneapolis, U.S.A.
Writer
Glen Wachowiak
Client
Lutheran Brotherhood

Art Director
Bert Gardner
Designer
Jeff Terwilliger
Design Agency
Bozell Inc.
Minneapolis, U.S.A.
Writer
Pete Pohl
Client
Lutheran Brotherhood

Art Director
Bert Gardner
Designer
Craig Tanimoto
Design Agency
Bozell Inc.
Minneapolis, U.S.A.
Writer
Glen Wachowiak
Client
Lutheran Brotherhood

Art Director
Bert Gardner
Designer
Craig Tanimoto
Design Agency
Bozell Inc.
Minneapolis, U.S.A.
Writer
Doug de Grood
Client
Lutheran Brotherhood

Art Directors
Al Fernandes/
Josh Portugal
Design Agency
Grey Advertising
San Francisco, U.S.A.
Photographer
Terry Heffernan
Writer
Bennett Miller
Typographer
Rapid Typographers
Client
Bank of America
Sign
Patrick Media Group

Creative Director
John Armistead
Art Director
Jeff Weekley
Design Agency
DMB&B
Los Angeles, U.S.A.
Photographer
Jeff Nadler Photography
Writer
Pieter Dreiband
Typographer
Amy Sanwald
Client
Security Pacific Bank
Sign
Patrick Media Group

Art Director
Frank Melf
Design Agency
Jacobson Rost
Sheboygan, U.S.A.
Writer
Dave Wood
Typographer
Jacobson Rost
Client
First Wisconsin Bank
Sign
Cramer Outdoor

177

Art Directors
Scott Willy/Dave Cranfill
Designer
Scott Willy
Design Agency
Cranfill Advertising
Agency
Indianapolis, U.S.A.
Illustrator
Scott Willy
Writer
Dave Cranfill
Typographer
Weimer Typesetting
Client
Farm Bureau Insurance
Sign
Naegele Outdoor
Advertising

Art Directors
Scott Willy/Dave Cranfill
Designer
Scott Willy
Design Agency
Cranfill Advertising
Agency
Indianapolis, U.S.A.
Illustrator
Scott Willy
Writer
Dave Cranfill
Typographer
Weimer Typesetting
Client
Farm Bureau Insurance
Sign
Naegele Outdoor
Advertising

Art Directors
Scott Willy/Dave Cranfill
Designer
Scott Willy
Design Agency
Cranfill Advertising
Agency
Indianapolis, U.S.A.
Illustrator
Scott Willy
Writer
Dave Cranfill
Typographer
Weimer Typesetting
Client
Farm Bureau Insurance
Sign
Naegele Outdoor
Advertising

Art Directors
Scott Willy/Dave Cranfill
Designer
Scott Willy
Design Agency
Cranfill Advertising
Agency
Indianapolis, U.S.A.
Illustrator
Scott Willy
Writer
Dave Cranfill
Typographer
Weimer Typesetting
Client
Farm Bureau Insurance
Sign
Naegele Outdoor
Advertising, Inc.

Art Director
Bruce Turkel
Designer
David Laidlaw
Design Agency
Turkel Laidlaw
Coconut Grove, U.S.A.
Illustrator
Henri Rousseau
Writers
Bruce Turkel/David
Laidlaw
Client
Mayfair
Sign
Ackerley
Communications

Art Directors
Constance Beck/
Terry P. Graboski
Designers
Constance Beck/
Terry P. Graboski
Design Agency
Beck&Graboski Design
Office
Santa Monica, U.S.A.
Writer
Terry P. Graboski
Typographer
Adcompositors
Client
Panda Management Co.
Sign
Patrick Media Group

Creative Director
Bill Borders
Art Director
Tim Parker
Designer
Tim Parker
Design Agency
Borders Perrin &
Norrander
Portland, U.S.A.
Writer
Greg Eiden
Typographer
BP&N Typesetting
Client
Red Lion Hotels & Inns

Bangkok for the Price of Baja ✈ Thai

ACKERLEY

Art Director
Sam Peck
Designer
Dale Lantz
Design Agency
Ackerley
Communications of the
Northwest, Inc.
Seattle, U.S.A.
Illustrator
Philip Howe
Writer
Sam Peck
Typographer
Typehouse
Client
Thai Airways
International
Sign
Ackerley
Communications of the
Northwest

Art Director
Kevin Shaw
Designer
Kevin Shaw
Design Agency
Travis Dale & Partners
London, England
Illustrator
Warren Maddill
Writer
Lawrence Pratt
Typographer
Kevin Shaw
Client
Royal Caribbean Cruise
Lines
Sign
Portland

Art Director
Jeff Layton
Designer
Jeff Layton
Design Agency
Grey Canada/Jeff Layton
& Assoc. Ltd.
Toronto, Canada
Photographer
Yuri Dojc
Writer
Mark Levine
Typographer
Typsettra
Client
Thomson Vacations
Sign
Mediacom Inc.

Art Director
Jeff Layton
Designer
Jeff Layton
Design Agency
Grey Canada/Jeff Layton
& Assoc. Ltd.
Toronto, Canada
Photographer
Yuri Dojc
Writer
Jeff Layton
Typographer
Typsettra
Client
Thomson Vacations
Sign
Mediacom Inc.

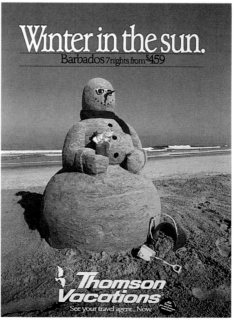

THE ENGLISH
RIVIERA
TORQUAY · PAIGNTON · BRIXHAM

Sanctuary Cove. Spectacular.
Splendid. Sportive. Sublime.
Salubrious. Special. Secure.

UTAH
FALL FOR IT

Art Director
Alan Lerner
Designer
Alan Lerner
Design Agency
Travis Dale & Partners
London, England
Illustrator
Brian Grimwood
Writer
Alan Lerner
Typographer
Alan Lerner
Client
Torbay Tourist Board
Sign
Portland

Art Director
Barrie Tucker
Designer
Barrie Tucker
Design Agency
Barrie Tucker Design Pty.
Ltd.
Adelaide, Australia
Writer
Barrie Tucker
Client
Sanctuary Cove
Gold Coast, Queensland
Sign
General Outdoor
Advertising

Art Director
Bob Wassom
Designer
Eric Bute
Design Agency
Harris & Love
Utah, U.S.A.
Writer
Bob Wassom
Typographer
Whipple
Client
Utah Travel Council

Art Directors
Scott Willy/
Dave Cranfill
Designer
Scott Willy
Design Agency
Cranfill Advertising
Agency
Indianapolis, U.S.A.
Illustrator
Scott Willy
Writer
Dave Cranfill
Typographer
Weimer Typesetting
Client
GTE North Classic
Client
Naegele Outdoor
Advertising

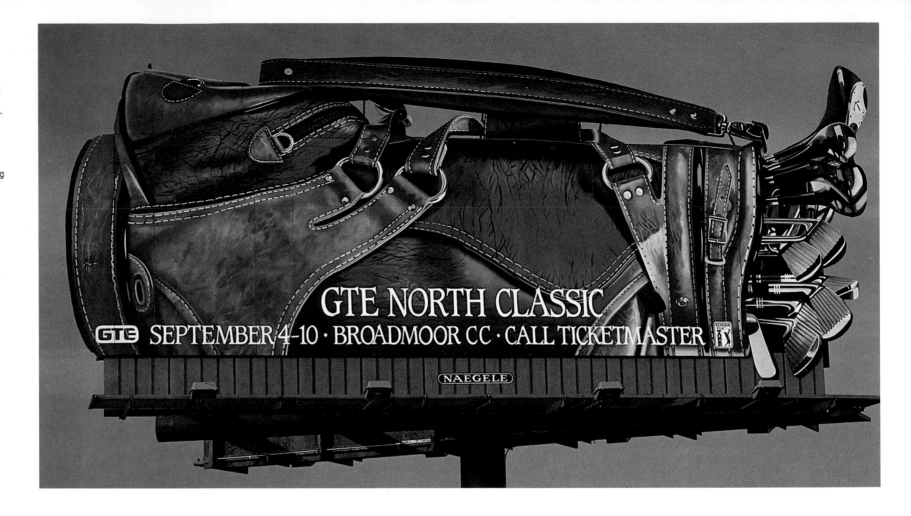

IT'S PARADISE WHICHEVER WAY YOU LOOK AT IT.

ROYAL CARIBBEAN ⚓ CRUISES

Doing time

bonjour
QUÉBEC

Out on probation

bonjour
QUÉBEC

Art Director
Terry Ross
Designer
Terry Ross
Design Agency
Travis Dale & Partners
London, England
Illustrator
Suc Young
Writer
Gill Sully
Typographer
Terry Ross
Client
Royal Caribbean Cruise
Line
Sign
Portland

Art Director
André Mantha
Design Agency
Groupe Morrow
Montréal, Canada
Illustrator
Handpainted in Detroit
Writer
Albert Martinaitis
Client
Ministère du Tourisme

Art Director
André Mantha
Design Agency
Groupe Morrow
Montréal, Canada
Photographer
Studio Cornellier
Writer
Albert Martinaitis
Typographer
M & H Typography
Client
Ministère du Tourisme
Quebec
Sign
Mediacom Inc.

Designer
Garry Emery
Design Agency
Emery Vincent Associates
South Melbourne,
Australia
Typographer
Garry Emery
Client
Powerhouse Museum

Art Directors
Fumihiko Enokido/
Hikaru Nagashita
Designer
Motoya Sugizaki
Design Agency
Fumihiko Enokido
Susono City, Japan
Illustrator
Fumihiko Enokido
Client
Livex Co. Ltd.

Art Director
Paul Dennis
Designer
Paul Dennis
Design Agency
Turner Design
South Perth, W. Australia
Client
Interstruct Holdings Ltd.
Sign
Rodan Design (Figures)
Australia Neon (Painting
& Lettering)

Art Director
Carl Smool
Designer
Carl Smool
Design Agency
Ackerley
Communications of the
Northwest
Seattle, U.S.A.
Client
"Flying City" Ackerley
Communications
Sign
Carl Smool & Ackerley
Communications

192

We're building another
Sunrise Preschool. Call 878-6556

Art Directors
Forrest & Valerie
Richardson
Design Agency
Richardson or
Richardson
Phoenix, U.S.A.
Typographer
Digitype
Client
Sunrise Preschools

Index of Creative Directors, Art Directors, Designers, Photographers, Illustrators, Writers and Typographers